new
trends
in
renovating

RoTo Architects Claudio Lazzarini
Oswald Mathias Ungers Brookes
Arima F. Delogu, G. Lixi, R. Consta
Claesson, Koivisto, Rune Vincent va
Berselli & Cecilia Cassina Mark Gu
Mastenbroek Kar-
Simon Cond
Architekten Ter
de Architecten
Mastenbroek)
Jean Nouvel A
Brown Mack
Mauro
3) M
Ge
Ko
W
Ru

& Carl Pickering Martin Wagner
Stacey Randall Rataplan Hiroyuki
ntini Studio Archea George Ranalli
n Duysen Fausto Colombo Ottorino
rd Architects Dick van Gameren &
Hwa Ho Jean-Paul Bonnemaison
r Julian Cowie Architects ARTEC
ver, Couvert & Beddock John Pawson
roep (Dick van Gameren & Bjarne
Beat Consoni Non Kitch Group bvba
maud Goujon Architecte DPLG Fraser
enna José Gigante Martin Wagner
Galantino & Federico Poli (Studio
Markus Wespi & Jérôme de Meuron
orges Maurios Kalhöfer &
schildgen Julia B. Bolles & Peter L.
son Christa Prantl & Alexander
ser Michael Graves Jo Crepain

new **trends** *in* renovating

Special edition for:

Gingko Press GmbH
Hamburger Strasse 180
D-22083 Hamburg
Germany

Phone: +49 (0)40 - 291 425
Fax: +49 (0)40 - 291 055
e-mail: gingkopress@t-online.de

Gingko Press Inc.
5768 Paradise Drive, Suite J
Corte Madera, CA 94925
USA

Phone: +1 - 415 - 924 9615
Fax: +1 - 415 - 924 9608
e-mail: books@gingkopress.com
www.gingkopress.com

Work conception: Carles Broto
Publisher: Arian Mostaedi

Graphic design & production: Pilar Chueca & Jorge Carmona
Text: Contributed by the architects, edited
*   by Jacobo Krauel and Amber Ockrassa*

© *Carles Broto i Comerma*
Jonqueres, 10, 1-5
08003 Barcelona, Spain
Tel.: +34 93 301 21 99 Fax: +34-93-301 00 21
E-mail: info@linksbooks.net

ISBN: 1-58423-195-5

Printed in Spain

new trends in renovating

Gingko Press

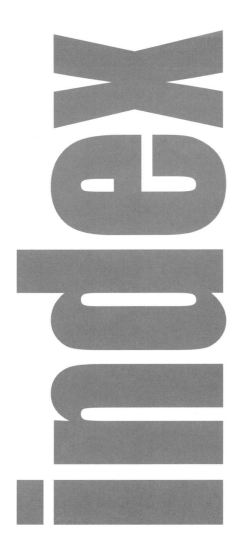

When it comes to renovating, there is no set of "right" or "wrong" criteria. Each project brings with it a unique combination of challenges, problems, strengths and weaknesses which have possibly never been seen before.

On historic buildings, how much of the old should be conserved? How far should the renovation either imitate or diverge from the original? What sort of new technologies and materials are compatible with old structures and finishes? These are just some of the questions which inevitably arise in renovating; and the best architects understand that the answers that apply in one project can never be re-used in subsequent programs. Everything must be reevaluated in light of the new challenges posed by new projects. The results of our search for some of the most exemplary work currently seen in the field of renovating are varied. Defunct factory buildings, centuries-old stone structures and elegant vaulted spaces are but some of the challenges facing the designers in this collection - all resolved with skill and artistry. From Arata Isozaki and Roberto Luno's masterful reworking of a modernist-era factory to the futuristic Lowe Apartment by Brookes Stacey Randall, a wide range of spaces and solutions is presented.

With this selection, we also hope to present a well-rounded vision of each project. To meet this end, we have endeavored to touch upon every aspect in the planning and renovation processes. After all, technical know-how is just as important as artistic vision in any project.

From conception to completion, we have included information on material used and construction processes in order to complement the ideas of the contributing architects. Finally, since nobody is in a better position to comment on these projects than the designers themselves, we have included the architects' own comments and anecdotes.

Therefore, we trust that we are leaving you in good, expert hands and that this selection of some of the finest, most innovative architectural solutions in the world will serve as an endless source of inspiration. Enjoy!

RoTo Architects
Carlson-Reges Residence

Los Angeles, USA

The owners built this dwelling, once an electric company facility, with materials from their salvage yard.

The clients wished to accommodate their expanding collection of paintings and sculptures to allow for occasional public showings without compromising the privacy of their living space. From the outset, the priorities of the architects shifted to the possibilities of volume and scale rather than the complexity or refinement of details.

An initial analysis of the site, the structure and the relation to the surrounding areas resulted in a series of constructed volumetric elements: the shield protects the translucent kitchen and the interior from the strongest southern sun, blocks the noise and dirt of the adjacent train switching yard, and forms a protected vertical garden.

The ground floor is used as semi-public garden and gallery spaces. A new exterior ground plane was created sixteen feet above grade and is contiguous to an elevated lap pool.

Cylindrical tanks from the client's materials yard were modified to make the pool that reflects the downtown skyline and a tower topped by a small garden belvedere.

The translational volume is supported by a wave-like truss system, which springs from a simple structural frame. Structurally, the new volume is completely independent to the existing shell and "mistakes" were never removed or rebuilt, but simply became the basis for the next set of decisions. In many instances, ideas were tested full size.

Photographs: Benny Chan / Fotoworks & Asassi productions

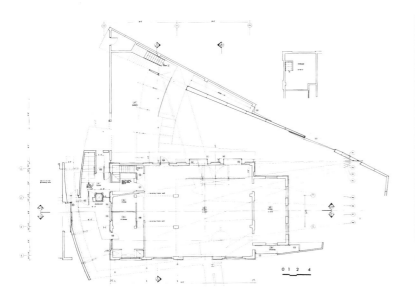

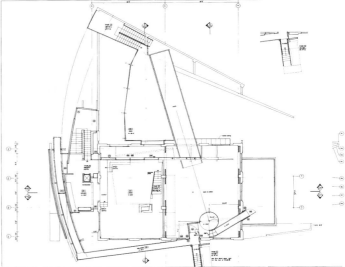

First floor plan   Second floor plan

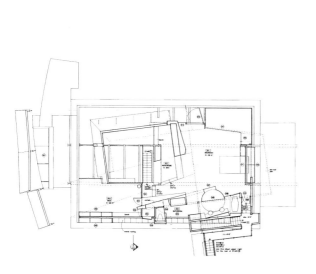

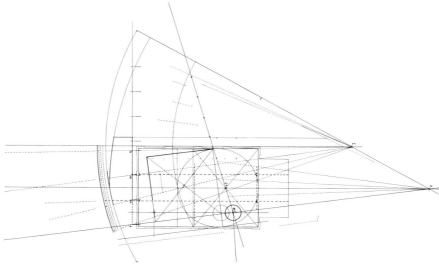

Third floor plan

The RoTo group of architects has been commissioned to remodel an old power station located in an active industrial area on the outskirts of Los Angeles.

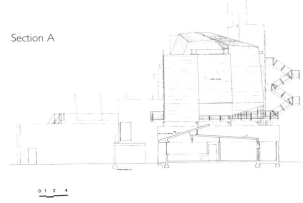

Section A

0 1 2 4

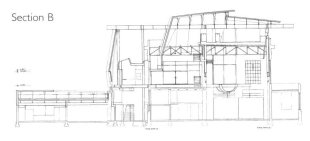

Section B

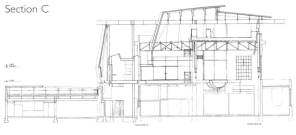

Section C

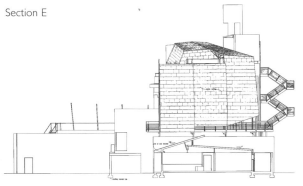

Section E

Cylindrical tanks from the clients' materials yard were modified to make the pool. As with the exterior, the interior features traditionally industrial materials such as concrete and steel.

Oswald Mathias Ungers
Wasserturm

Utscheid, Germany

The original tower dating from 1957 had only the two upper floors, housing the water tank and machinery, and a high entrance hall. The kitchen floor is a new addition, and is over-looked by a gallery running parallel to the stairs. On the first level is a newly constructed element containing the bedroom with shower, bath and fitted cupboards. The top floor is a tall space with four windows. Sparsely furnished, it is a meditation area with breathtaking views of the Eifel Mountains.

Entering the tower, one is struck by the succession of spaces that have been created: the alternation of wide-narrow and high-low. Emerging from the low, narrow stairwell there is a high, wide space with a view of the landscape.

The spaces in the water tower are simple elements stacked one on top of the other, but the artistry of the design lay in the adapting and refining the existing aesthetics to the new use. The spaces and materials are thus left in their purest form: sandstone, the circular form of the steps, the verticality of the layout, the new additions. All is pure, unobtrusive, natural.

An example of this is that the windows largely follow the original design, serving less an idea of living space and views, and more the original purpose of illumination: one window on the stairwell, one in the kitchen and one in the bathroom. However, on the second floor the situation is different. Four windows point in the four directions, thus adding a new dimension to the circular plan thanks to the conceptual rigor of the architect, who pursued the maxim "Less is more" with laudable sensitivity.

Photographs: Stefan Müller

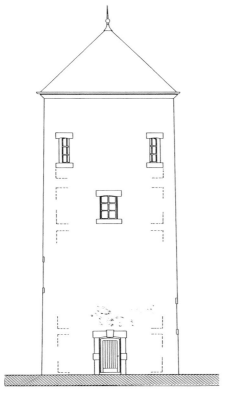

Main facade

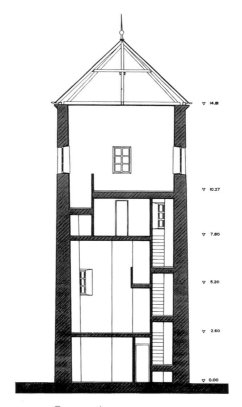

Cross-section

The project has used the existing openings except on the top floor, in which four new windows look out in the four directions.

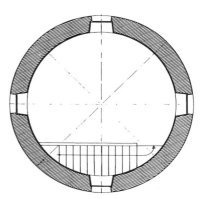

Third floor plan

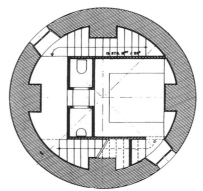

Second floor plan

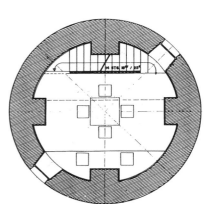

First floor plan

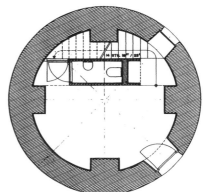

Ground floor plan

Brookes Stacey Randall
Lowe Apartment

London, UK

Brookes Stacey Randall were commisioned to create a "calm and light interior space" within the top small floor of a converted warehouse. The form of the existing shell was a very particular half arch with a small side space. A potential roof terrace was separated from the main volume and accessed via a lower terrace and a spiral staircase.

The main volume was treated as a room whose function can change depending on the particular facilities brought into use. In order to achieve this, the small side space was split into storage and bathroom areas.

The storage area was equipped with three large pull-out "pods", each providing a different faclity for the main space. Each pod was designed to cantilever out on a triple extending mechanism, similar to that of a filing cabinet drawer.

Directly above the center of the space, a curved double glazed rooflight opens on hidraulic arms.

The circulation within the flat has been designed to maximize a sense of scale, alternately concealing and revealing views as the user moves through the space. The convergent curved wall lead the user from the dim entrance toward the light of the main space whilst the route broadens and the height increases towards the the curved ceiling rising above.

Photographs: Katsuhisha Kida

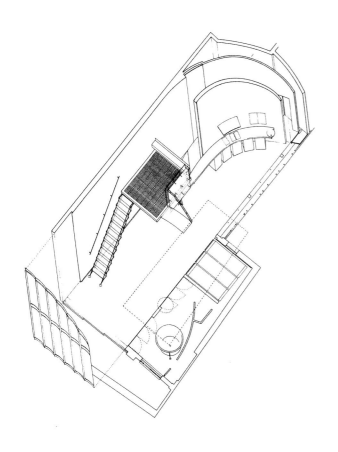

Interior elevation

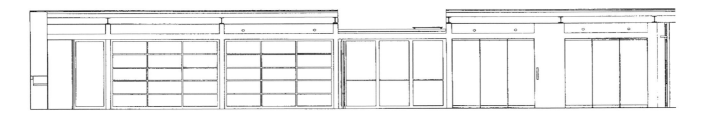

Upper level floor plan

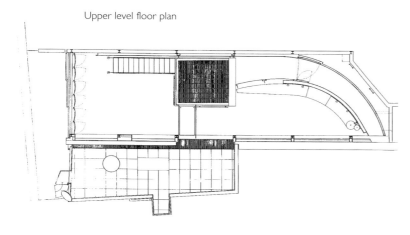

Longitudinal section

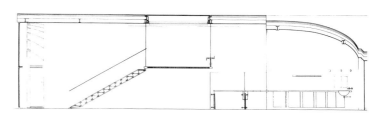

Lower level floor plan

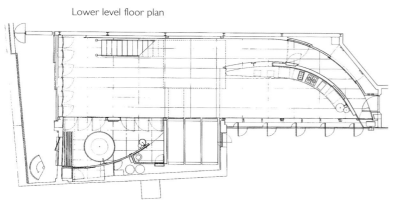

Cross section

Cristian Cirici & Carles Bassó
Vapor Llull

Barcelona, Spain

The Vapor Llull (a steam-driven factory), in an old industrial district of Barcelona, consisted of a set of buildings dating from the early 20th century which had been used for manufacturing chemical products. The basic structure of the complex consisted of a long ground floor plus two floors, the highest of which had a sloping roof supported by a structure of wooden trusses. The complex also included a series of auxiliary premises adjoining the main building and a magnificent brick chimney measuring over thirty meters in height that was part of the steam engine that once powered the factory. The architects decided to conserve the chimney as a way of recalling a time in which this district was filled with steam-driven factories.

The most suitable property for conversion into loft dwellings was the long main building. In order to create an open, private space and provide a one-vehicle parking space for each of the eighteen units into which the scheme was subdivided, a series of auxiliary buildings were demolished.

To give independent access to each module of approximately 90 m², three sets of vertical communication elements were introduced, each with a stairwell and a panoramic elevator. Their formal expression gives the appearance of silos covered with enamelled corrugated steel. On the outside the main building was painted with silicate paint applied directly to the bricks, which were first stripped of their render.

In the interior, the spaces were left open and unfinished, so that each loft could be arranged according to the wishes of the different designers that were chosen to finish off the scheme. The layout and decor of this loft is by Inés Rodríguez. It is a two-level apartment in which a mezzanine houses the bedroom and a bathtub. It is a curious habitat in which the light and the space create an atmosphere of elegance.

Photographs: Rafael Vargas

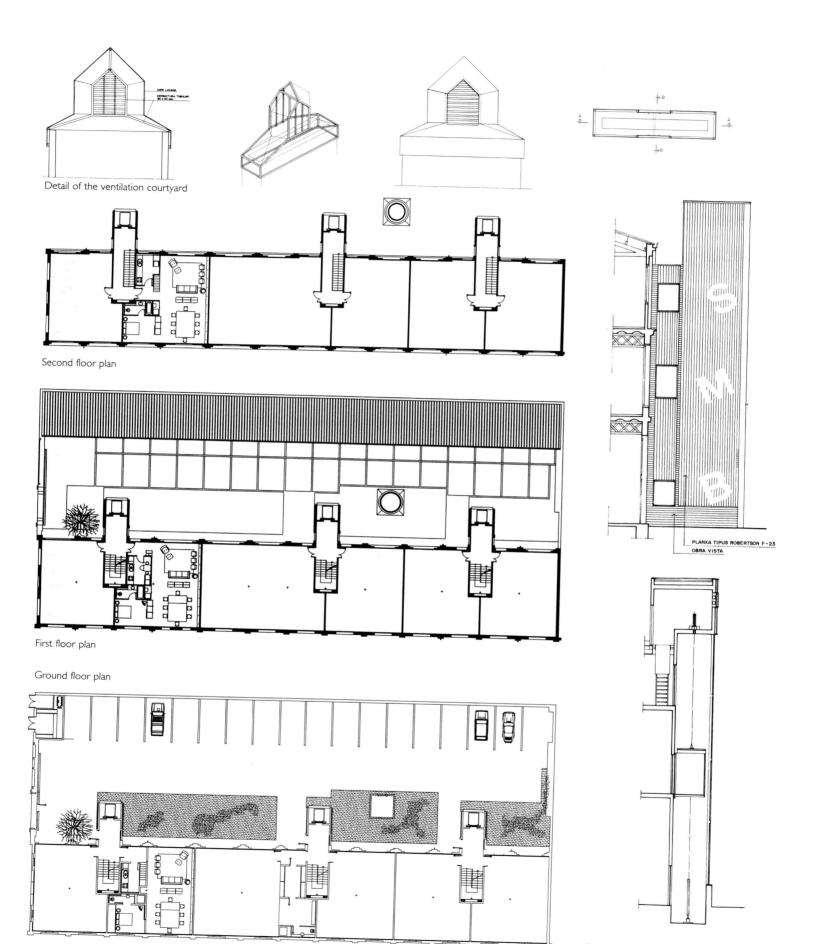

Detail of the ventilation courtyard

Second floor plan

First floor plan

Ground floor plan

PLANXA TIPUS ROBERTSON F-23
OBRA VISTA

Panoramic detail of elevator windows

Claudio Lazzarini & Carl Pickering
Residence on the Sicilian Coast

Sicily, Italy

In this conversion of a 19th-century villa in south-eastern Sicily into a contemporary holiday home, the client wanted a new interior (a landing with three rooms, two bathrooms and stairs overlooking a sitting room) in an existing space with a double-height ceiling.

The intense Sicilian light glancing off local stone immediately imposed itself as a central theme. The villa's roof was opened to bring light into all the floors through skylights that are screened by external blinds in summer. To mark out the new windows on the elevations (loopholes landward, large ports seaward) the stone of the walls was dematerialized by a chamfer.

Inside, the staircase is a scroll of blackened steel set in a cylindrical volume that forms a well of light, the pivot of a natural air-conditioning system that refers to Arab and Norman vernacular. An eight-centimeter slit in the central wall of the living-room runs up eight meters to the terrace. It is toplit and throws a tracer blade of light into the room during the day, which varies its swath according to the seasons like a sundial.

Like an ode to Mediterranean light and the sea wind this project, which was two years in the making, is a manifesto: the elegance of its honed spaces is rounded out by elaborate yet discreet details.

The villa is a concentrate of the architects' love for the stone of the south and the refined use of poor traditional materials. It bears witness to their skill in inventing or reinterpreting highly functional construction systems in an artistic way.

Photographs: Giovanna Cipparrone

BB Cross-section

The new openings on the exterior of the villa take the form of small narrow cracks. They are thus distinguished and are superimposed clearly on the existing openings without altering the general image of the building.

AA Cross-section

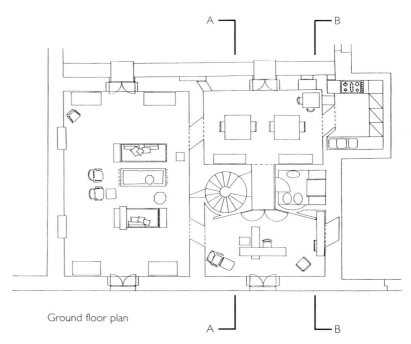

Ground floor plan

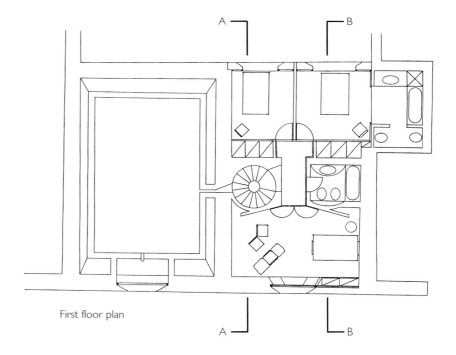

First floor plan

The elegance and sobriety of the interior spaces, in which the use of traditional material prevails, is compensated by small details that are elaborated and discreet. Here, images of the crack in the central wall of the living-room.

The dematerialization of the bevelled angles, the unexpected cuts in the walls, the skylights and the angled openings create unexpected perspectives of the interior of the dwelling and allow a greater connection between rooms with minimum modifications to the original structure.

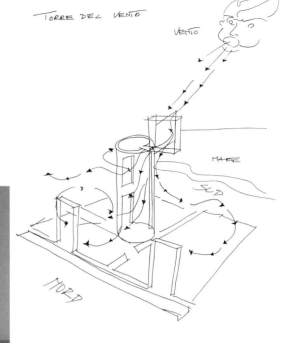

TORRE DEL VENTO

VENTO

MARE

SUD

NORD

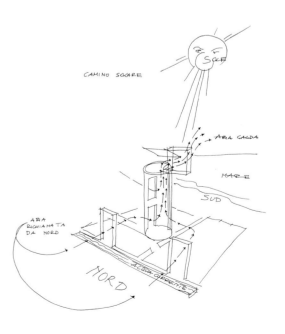

CAMINO SOLARE

SOLE

ARIA CALDA

MARE

SUD

ARIA
RICHIAMATA
DA NORD

NORD

George Ranalli
K-loft

New York City, USA

This project was for the renovation of a loft in New York City for two artists and their son.

The existing space was a room with exposed brick bearing walls running the lenght of the space and a brick ceiling with a series of vaults spanning steel sections from the front to the back of the loft. The plan called for two new bedrooms, a new master bathroom, a new kitchen, and a second bathroom. It was also the owners' intention that the feeling and quality of the original loft be maintained.

The solution as built features a series of volumes sitting in the loft which allow the space of the room to be continuous. Each of the volumes takes a key position so that it contains space as well as producing space between the forms. The elements are made in plaster which then have some fixed translucent glass inserted in the blocks. These glass openings are meant to allow the passage of light and space from one room to another. The corners are protected with large panels of of birch plywood cut in irregular profiles that gives an expressive value to these volumes. These panels are fixed to the plaster walls with a pattern of screw fasteners. All doors, lamps, cabinets, and other decorative objects are custom-designed as part of the project.

The project was designed and built in materials of a high finish to accentuate and contrast the rough container of the existing brick room. The main structure and surface of the new elements is frame and skimcoat gypsum board that gives a smooth, durable finish to the new shapes.

Photographs: Paul Warchol

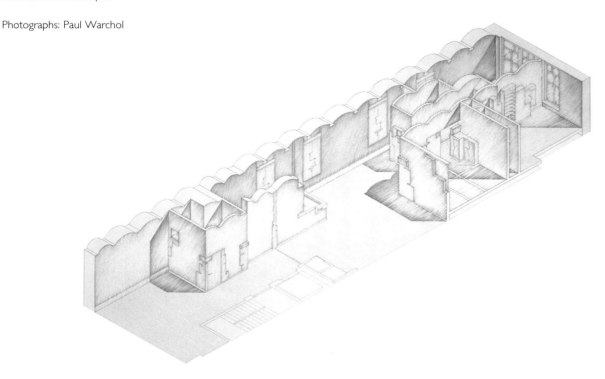

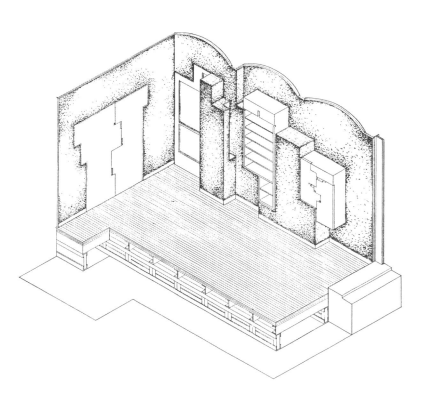

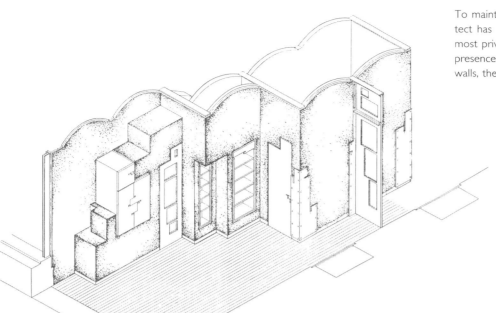

To maintain the impression of a single open space, the architect has implanted a series of isolated volumes in which the most private rooms are located. Thus, thanks to the constant presence of magnificent vaulted ceramic ceilings and red brick walls, the sensation of continuity is constant.

Vincent van Duysen
Finca in Mallorca

Mallorca, Spain

This house maintains the characteristics and spirit of the original Majorcan vernacular architecture on the outside, while creating a contemporary image on the inside.

The project began with an old country house in the inland part of the island with a theatrical portico of the main facade and two adjacent buildings that function as the custodian's lodging and the owner's office. Van Duysen also worked on the design of the garden, creating visual connections by means of paving in a particular composite of concrete and local stone, also used for the flooring of the buildings to create a sense of indoor-outdoor continuity. An imposing wooden enclosure defines a true barrier, both physical and visual, between the private residential space and the custodian's lodging, or between the interior and exterior worlds.

As visitors cross the threshold they have the impression of entering a large patio, which is nevertheless intimate and welcoming. The only theatrical presence in this space is a wash-stand made of a single block of stone, inserted in a niche. This sensation continues inside the main house. The entrance area is an empty room, with wood paneling on the walls, concealing the access to the guest bathroom. From the entrance one proceeds to the large kitchen/dining room or to the staircase leading to the upper level housing the bedrooms.

The rigor of the furnishing solutions for each room, based on simple planes and elementary volumes, solids and space, elements for storage and display, seems to make reference to a monastic model of living. The sensory richness of the materials used (sanded and stained oak, stone, marble, ceramics) gives these solutions an air of extreme elegance. Meticulous attention was paid to detail and to the choice of delicate color combinations to create a relaxing atmosphere for this holiday home.

Photographs: Alberto Piovano

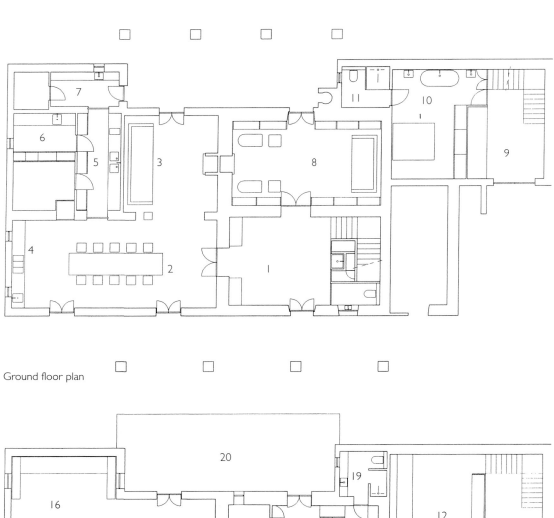

Ground floor plan

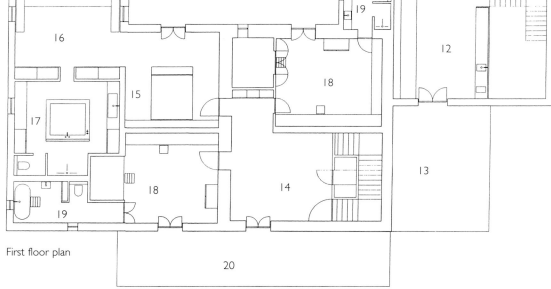

First floor plan

1. Main entrance
2. Dining room
3. Living room
4. Kitchen
5. Scullery
6. Laundry
7. Back entrance
8. Library
9. Guesthouse entrance
10. Guesthouse bedroom & bathroom

11. Guesthouse shower
12. Guesthouse kitchen
13. Guesthouse terrace
14. Nighthall
15. Master bedroom
16. Dressing master bedroom
17. Master bathroom
18. Child's bedroom
19. Child's bathroom
20. Mainhouse terrace

The architecture of Vicent van Duysen is based on premises such as simplicity and comfort, with a predominance of pure lines and an unadorned architecture. He thus builds exquisite spaces in which the light and the soft colors play a major role.

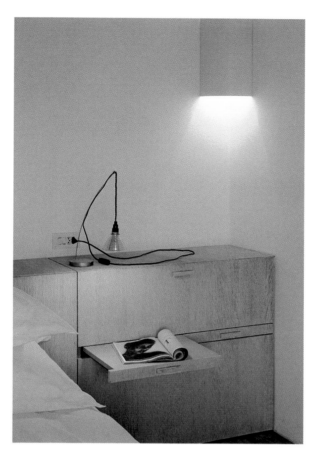

The washbasin located in the entrance area is housed in a natural wooden closet located at the bottom of the staircase leading to the upper floor.

Studio Archea
House in Costa San Giorgio

Florence, Italy

This apartment is located in an old medieval tower near the Ponte Vecchio, in the heart of Florence. The original Renaissance building had large wooden beams that gave it a certain majesty, and the challenge consisted in designing a residential space that took advantage of the exceptional characteristics of the quattrocento to create a functional and contemporary atmosphere.

The space is designed around a curvilinear stone wall that organizes the diverse functions of the dwelling and supports the metal beams of the mezzanine, and which is used as the bedroom. This wall acts as a bookcase, leaves the kitchen semi-concealed, houses the stairwell in its perimeter, and divides the spaces so that the materials define and organize the different atmospheres of the dwelling. An iron staircase set against the opposite wall leads to a platform giving access to the mezzanine. From this horizontal platform, a walkway also leads to a small panoramic pool over the dining room with a bathroom next to it. This area of the upper floor is in the new stone part of the apartment; the rectilinear mezzanine is separated by a small wooden floor space.

Because of the small size of the scheme, the architects were able to design all the elements in detail, avoiding prefabrication and creating unique, almost sculptural objects.

The architects showed great respect for tradition in the use of natural stone, in the conservation of the original ceiling and in the distribution of the furniture. A single space and different atmospheres for one person: this is the result of this intervention in an apartment set between walls full of history.

Photographs: Alessandro Ciampi

The void created between the two main volumes is used as a corridor on the ground floor. On the upper floor, this free space offers different views and perspectives, and opens up the dimensions of the apartment.

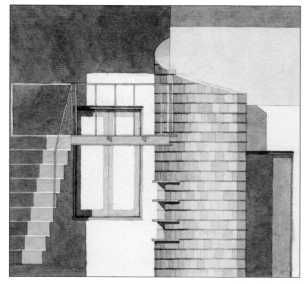

Rataplan
Bürombau Vienna Paint

Wien, Austria

An industrial workshop dating from 1899 was converted to provide the offices of a digital company. The commission was to contain workstations, computer room, scanner room, film processing equipment, etc. all cross-linked. Each of these fields also had to correspond to different requirements of acoustics, lighting and climate.

It was a very important starting point of the architectural concept to create no cells but to conserve the originally open space and to generate views.

On the first floor there are offices, an exhibition space on the ground floor and a coffee house in an annex. The entrance area is marked by a horizontal steel plate that acts as a canopy and draws visitors into the space. A new staircase leads to the upper level where the offices are located. This staircase is formulated as an upright element linking the two floors. The existing elevator was partly exposed by removing a wall and part of the ceiling. The windows have been enlarged and transformed; now they give views of the industrial chimney and allow it to function inside the space.

In the upper floor the horizontal composition remains, by means of three freestanding, articulated shelf elements. As with all new additions in the building, these elements are set at an angle of 11° to the existing walls, forming the backbone of the space and accentuating the perspective. All abutments to the existing walls and roof are in glass to maintain the sense of spatial continuity.

On account of the different requirements, it had to be possible to close off the individual areas. Between the closed areas are the "work bays" of the zones without special acoustic and climatic requirements. The office in the middle of the space represents the 'market place' where clients are received.

Photographs: Markus Tomaselli

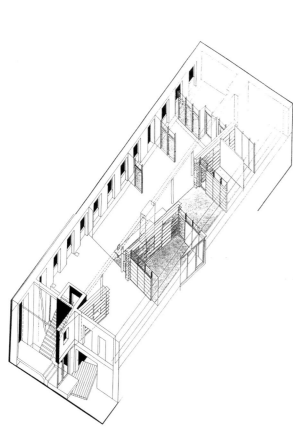

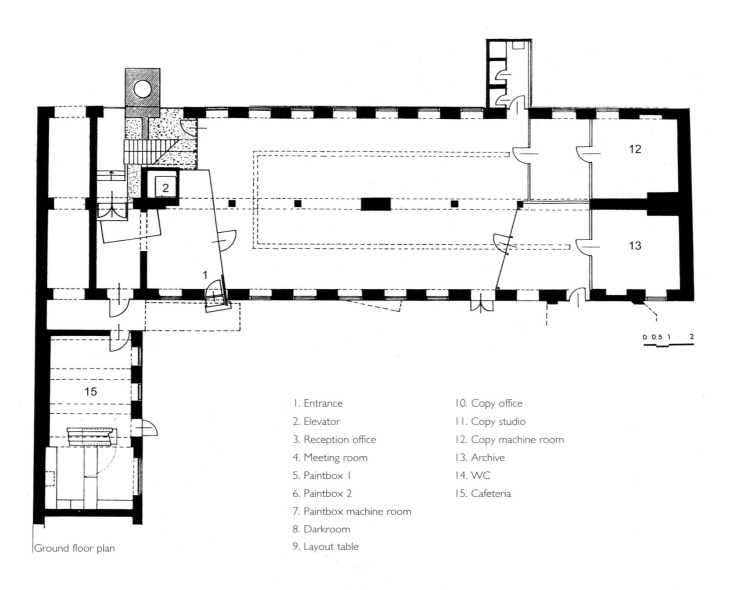

Ground floor plan

1. Entrance
2. Elevator
3. Reception office
4. Meeting room
5. Paintbox 1
6. Paintbox 2
7. Paintbox machine room
8. Darkroom
9. Layout table

10. Copy office
11. Copy studio
12. Copy machine room
13. Archive
14. WC
15. Cafeteria

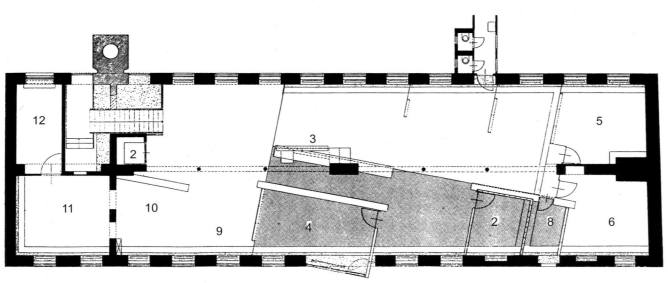

First floor plan

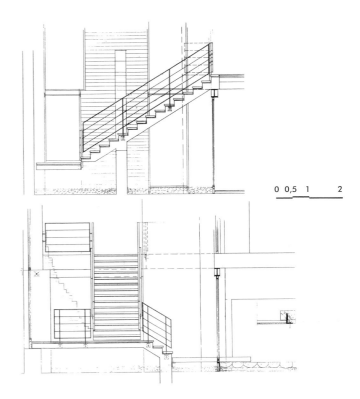

0 0,5 1 2

Three self-supporting shelving units placed at an angle of 11°
against the walls of the building articulate the space and accentuate the effect of perspective. The elements of glass and perforated metal plate appear alternately transparent or opaque
according to the given lighting conditions.

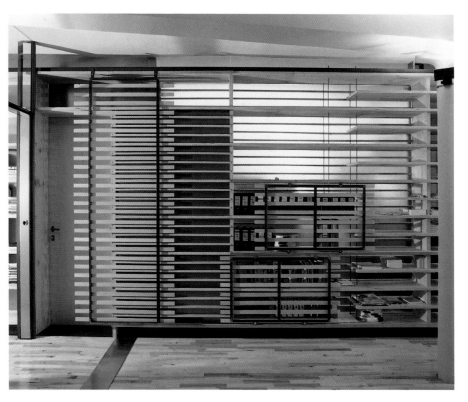

Hiroyuki Arima
House 3R

Fukuoka, Japan

The building is located some distance from the city center on a site studded with different kinds of trees such as maple and cherry, whose aspect varies with the seasons.

The scheme is a conversion of a small old apartment house to provide a favorable environment for living. Although there was nothing particularly unique about the 20-year-old building, a residential law banned any alterations to the outer appearance. The structures are on a northern slope with the front road on the third floor level, and access to the maisonette is possible only by going underground by stairs at road level.

"3r" (3 reeds) means three units of a movable wooden wall panel which is deployed near the entrance of the maisonette. Since the three units revolve independently of each other, it is possible for a resident to select diverse spatial variations. There are no specific restrictions governing the spatial configuration.

The former interior furnishings in the space have all been demolished and the floors, walls and ceilings are all painted white to make the most of the weak sunlight on the north side. The entire space constitutes a huge continuous structure.

Several necessary functions, such as the installation area, bedroom and sanitary rooms, are deployed continuously along two floors while being connected by a stairwell. The outer walls with the existing sash windows are all covered with translucent plastic panels from the inside. Holes in a variety of diameters have been punched into the surface of the wooden and plastic panels.

Photographs: Koji Okamoto

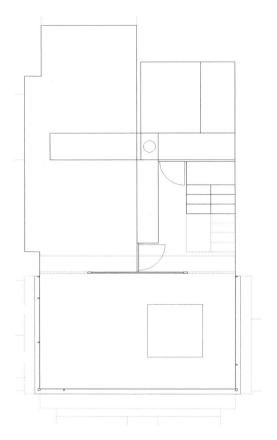

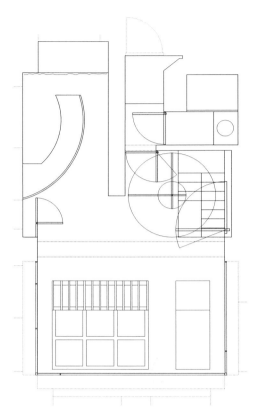

Upper floor plan

First floor plan

The surfaces that enclose the apartment's floors, walls and roof were painted white in order to reflect and multiply the scarce light from the north that penetrates through the existing openings. These were clad in translucent plastic panels.

Though it is organized on two different floors, the apartment constitutes a single continuous space, thereby offering a wide variety of visual perspectives.

A steep slender stairway with a metal skeleton and wooden steps communicates the floor that gives access to the dwelling with the lower level on which most of the private rooms are located.

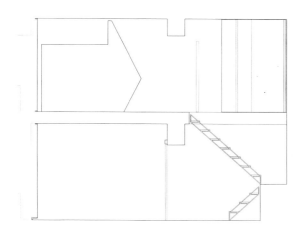

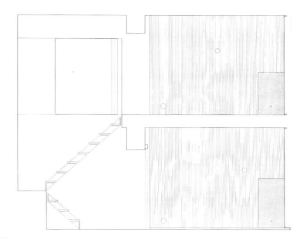

Cross-sections

The wide range of positions of the three mobile wooden panels provide the owner with numerous options for configuring the space.

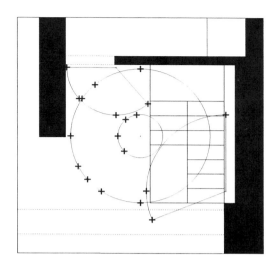
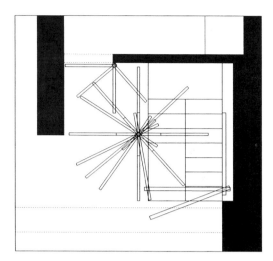

F. Delogu, G. Lixi, R. Constantini & H. Andreeva
Borgo di Sacrofano

Sacrofano, Italy

Located a few kilometers north of Rome, the Borgo di Sacrofano is a small agricultural center of medieval origin that sits silently in the residential fabric of the city: a disordered agglomerate of small residential units piled on top of each other, distributed around a small central square and aligned along the main street of the town.

The project was to restructure one of these units, located on the first floor of a building that looks directly onto the plaza. This unit was originally subdivided into four adjacents square parts and only lit on two sides that featured few windows. The architectural idea that guided the intervention was the desire to join the original environments in a single common and continuous space, in which light plays a unifying role, an Ariadne's thread that places each architectural element in connection, suggesting keys to the reading and emphasizing the peculiar elements of the composition. By day, the light arrives mainly through the large skylights, while at night it is regulated by means of an electric system that adapts the internal illumination to the external conditions.

A system of two orthogonal wall axes intertwines the atmospheres, cutting new volumes that are independent of the original walls; each element fits into the adjoining one, and forms, material and colors come closer and move away in a sequence of elements that shapes the project by means of a single system integrated into the original structure.

Photographs: Roberto Bossaglia

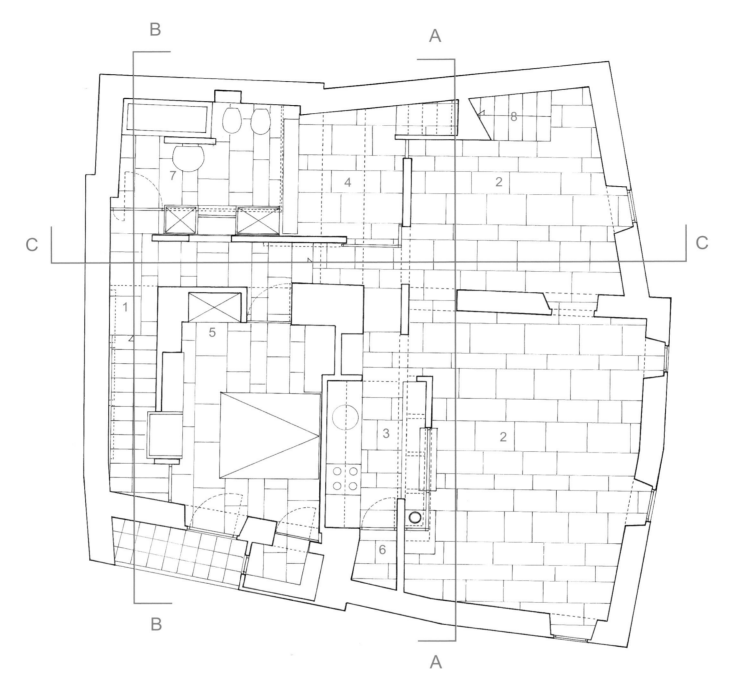

Ground floor plan

1. Entrance
2. Living-room
3. Kitchen
4. Office
5. Bedroom
6. Storage
7. Bathroom
8. Stairs to balcony

The apartment has been floored in stone and its walls have been stuccoed in a range of textures and colours. Furnishings are entirely in mahogany wood.

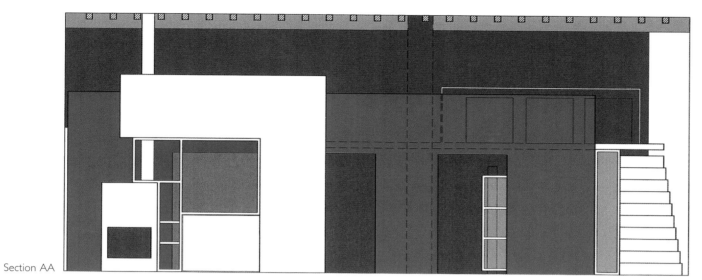

Section AA

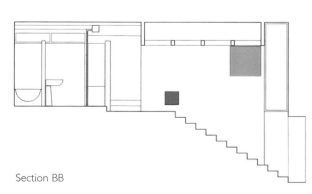

Section BB

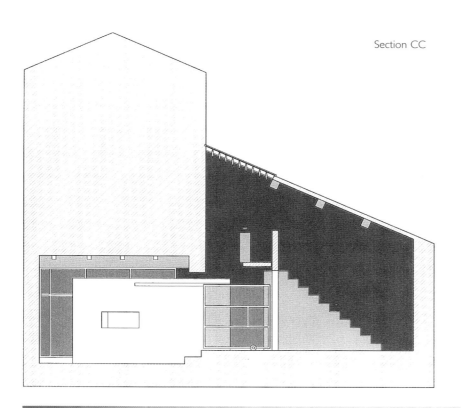

Section CC

Dick van Gameren & Mastenbroek
Kantoor in Penthouse

Amsterdam, The Netherlands

The project is focused on the restoration of part of three canal houses on the Keizersgracht to serve the needs of the Dutch branch of an international computer company. The office takes up the first floor of a large townhouse that had been created from the amalgamation of three canal houses. The original interiors have disappeared, and the breaking down of the walls and leveling out of differences in height between the buildings have damaged the original layout.

Additions have been treated through the position, the connections and the usage of materials as new elements that do not hide the historical body of the building.

The conversion of the office was the beginning of a plan for the total renovation of the complex. The main concerns were the improvement of the relationship with the spacious back garden (designed by Mien Ruys) and the addition of a number of bedrooms and a second kitchen.

Photographs: Rick Klein Gotink

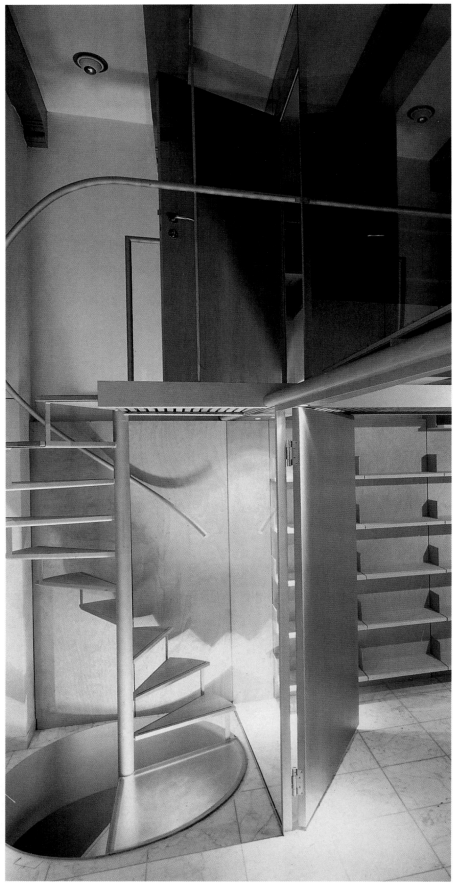

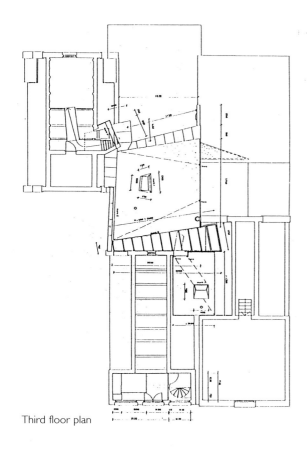

Third floor plan

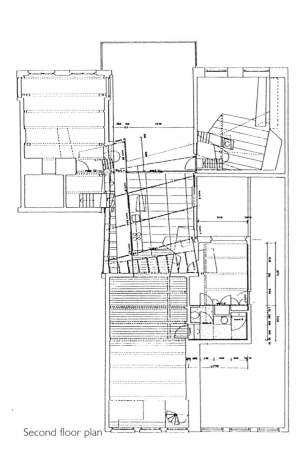

Second floor plan

81

The project establishes new channels of vertical communication by mean of a metal spiral staircase, the directional nature of which is underlined by a light banister rail.

The work was done in such a way that the installation of new materials and the creation of new connections do not conceal the original structures of the historical building.

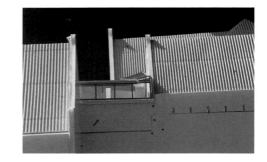

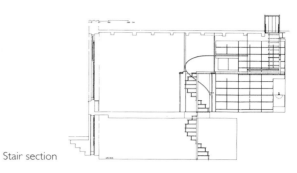

Stair section

Mark Guard Architects
Refurbishment of a House in Kensal Rise
London, UK

The original building, a car repair shop, consisted of a two-story brick structure with garages covered in pitched roofing on each side. The architects' mission was to create a two-bedroom house in this building. By removing the rudimentary roofing, they created an entrance court on one side and a walled garden on the other.

To provide views of Saint Paul's church and Greenwich, bays were opened in the east facade, and the living room and kitchen were placed on the upper floor. The bedrooms on the ground floor open onto the garden. The wall is replaced by sliding window partitions: on the ground floor and on the upper floor, these panels can slide completely to open the space onto the garden. In the studio, glass panels can also disappear in order to eliminate all limits between the inside and the outside. The architects tried to explore the possibilities of a garden on two levels with views of every floor in order to connect the living-room with the roof terrace of the studio. Independent concrete walls define the spaces inside the garden and support the steel reinforcement beams of the existing structure and the frames of the sliding bays.

An axis joining the entrance court to the garden through the house is underlined by a strip of water and a new door in the enclosed garden, which is the end of the axis and may also serve as an independent entrance to the studio. A walkway will later join the living-room to the studio terrace. At the top of the staircase a glass bench accentuates the transparency and preserves the visual relationship between the ground floor and the lounge. The floors are in rough concrete, a subtle reference to the gravel of the garden. The walls are treated as white screens and the narrow kitchen is clad in stainless steel like a ship's kitchen. All interior and exterior doors, and even the shutters, are sliding.

Photographs: : John Edward Linden / Arcaid

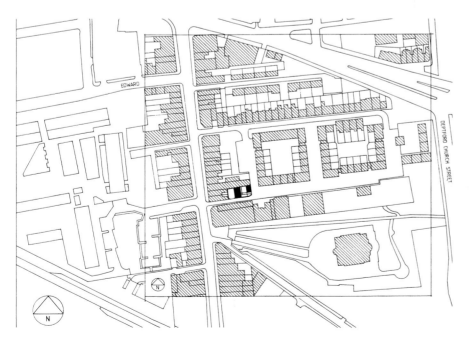

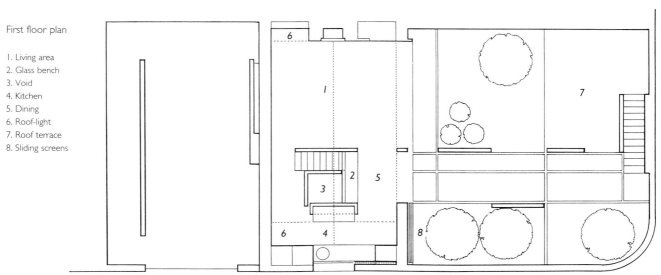

First floor plan

1. Living area
2. Glass bench
3. Void
4. Kitchen
5. Dining
6. Roof-light
7. Roof terrace
8. Sliding screens

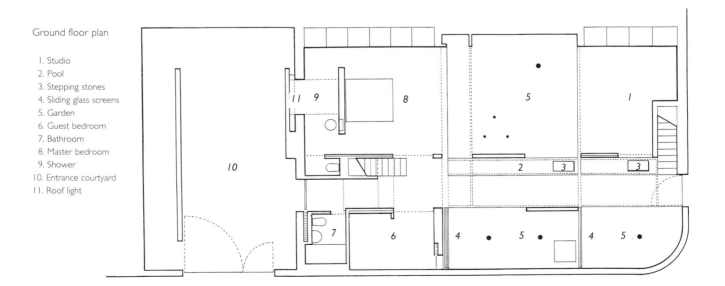

Ground floor plan

1. Studio
2. Pool
3. Stepping stones
4. Sliding glass screens
5. Garden
6. Guest bedroom
7. Bathroom
8. Master bedroom
9. Shower
10. Entrance courtyard
11. Roof light

North elevation

South elevation

Ottorino Berselli & Cecilia Cassina
Residenza in Puegnago del Garda

Monte Acuto, Italy

In the Italian hills of Valtenesi, overlooking Lake Gada stands the small town of Monte Acuto. It is presided over by a tower with an old dovecote, a construction typical of the plain of Padania but uncommon in this region.

The restoration project covered one corner of the old town, which dates backs to the end of the sixth century and is dominated by the massive quadrangular tower. The whole complex was in an advanced state of disrepair, particularly the tower, and a thorough restoration was therefore carried out on several levels. The project was based on the idea of retrieving previously existing elements, with particular attention to interpreting everything that, through the successive layers that had been superimposed over the years, bore clear indications of its past. The project therefore proposed a reassessment of the whole town, despite the fact that it directly affected only a fragment of it, "in an attempt to regain lost urban emotions", in the words of the authors in their report on the project.

The theme running through the new work is light, which assumes the main role in the scheme as a result of the generous yet subtle openings. The serene atmosphere of the interior of the old tower (now converted into a dwelling) is bathed in light entering through clean slits running the length of the ceiling on the first two floors, where the main rooms are situated.

The material used (palette-applied intonaco on the walls, and colored cement and natural oak on the floors) endow all the rooms with a homogenous feel. The distribution of the rooms was problematic due to the unusual structure of the house, particularly the top story, formerly used as a dovecote. Finally the solutions adopted were to use the ground floor as the bedrooms. The remaining floors (the second and third level and the former dovecote) contain the guest rooms, various study areas and a library, with panoramic views of the lake.

Photographs: Alberto Piovano

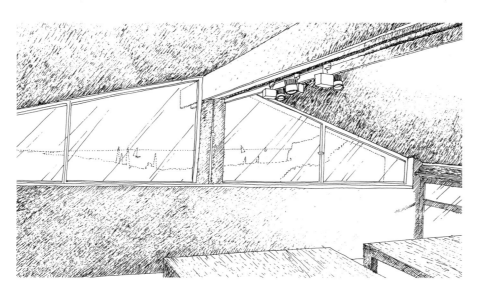

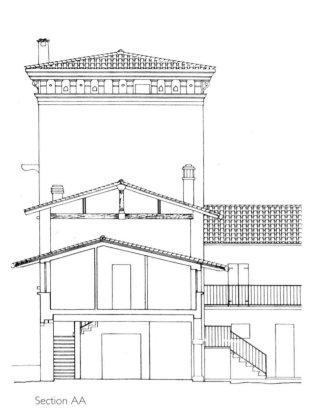

Section AA

91

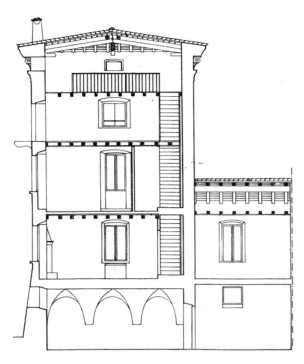

Section BB

The project involved the restoration and renovation of an old building characterized by a tower crowned with a dovecote. Now converted into a dwelling, before the reparation the complex was in an advanced state of disrepair.

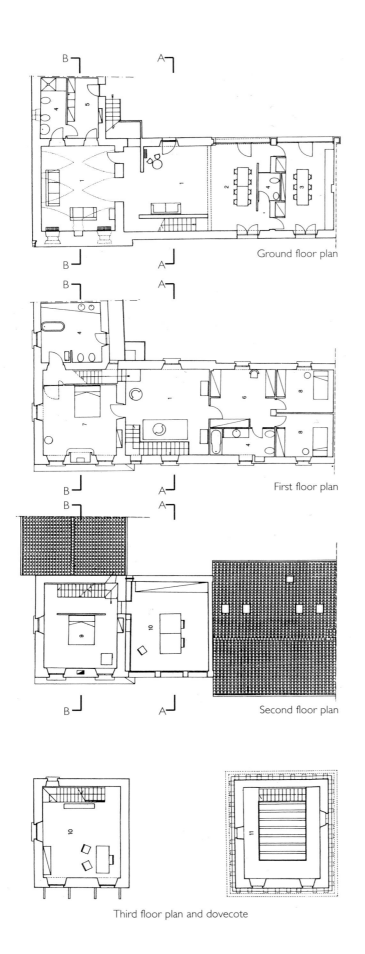

Ground floor plan

First floor plan

Second floor plan

Third floor plan and dovecote

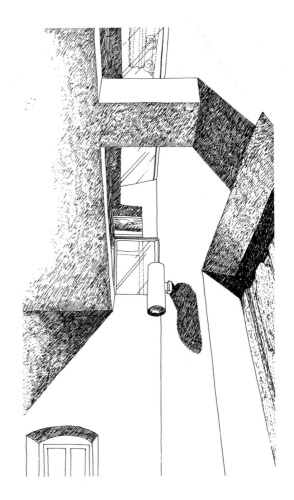

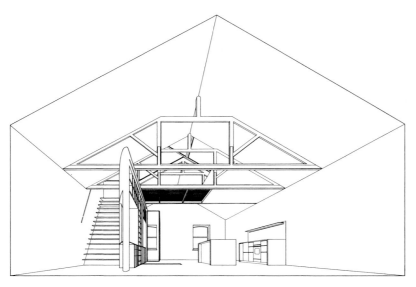

Simon Conder
Residential conversion of a fire station

London, UK

The clients, a musician and a chef, had bought the top two floors of the obsolete Holland Park Fire Station. Although the building was in a quite tree-lined street, the actual accommodation consisted of a number of small, badly lit rooms with those at the back overshadowed by the adjacent property sitting only 3.5 meters away from the rear wall.

The depth of the plan was particularly dark. The clients' main objective was to find an imaginative way of transforming this rather depressing environment into a light and exciting new home which would have a generosity of scale and spirit.

On a more detailed level they wanted a solution that would incorporate an open plan living area, the heart of which was to be the kitchen, a large main bedroom with an en-suite bathroom, two smaller bedrooms (one of which was to double as a study). An additional bathroom, and a large amount of built-in storage for clothes and the clients' large collection of records and compact discs.

At roof level, there were dramatic views out over West London and it was clear that the building could be transformed if this rooftop potential could be exploited to create an additional living space and let natural light down into the center of the exceptionally deep spaces below.

The final solution was based on three key elements: a roof top conservatory, a flight of stone steps and three-story storage wall. The roof of the conservatory can retract in good weather to create an open roof terrace. This steel and glass structure allows sunlight to flood down into the center of the second floor living area, and a section of glass floor at this level also allows natural light to penetrate down to the first floor hallway below. The grand flight of tapering stone steps leads directly from the front door street level up to the second floor living area. The storage wall both defines the staircase and separates it from the accommodation at first and second levels.

Photographs: C. Gascoine / VIEW

It was the owners' explicit wish that the main elements in the open-plan living room should be the kitchen, located in a central position, and a structure for storing their large collection of records and CDs. The central part was paved in translucent glass to bring light up from below.

The lack of natural light, a direct consequence of the small size of the openings, was counteracted through the use of light, translucent materials.

Claesson Koivisto Rune
Private apartment / Town house

Stockholm, Sweden

The team of architects Marten Claesson, Eero Koivisto and Ola Rune were contracted to restore two apartments in the center of Stockholm.

In the first one, for a young manager with little free time, they attempted to organize a peaceful home for "charging the batteries" after long working days and trips. This dwelling is located in a late 19th century building with a wooden floor.

Half was kept in its original state (this corresponded to the living room), while the rest of the rooms (the bedroom, kitchen and bathroom) were modernized. In order to further emphasize the contrast between the two areas, the new area was painted pale gray and the original area was painted white.

The floor plan was devised in order to create visual fluidity between the rooms. To communicate the spaces in a simple and functional way, two new structures were designed. A curved corner leads from the entrance into the first axis along the bathroom, kitchen and bedroom. The second axis of intersection runs from the kitchen to the dining room, where a wall with a hatch was built.

The final result was a comfortable apartment full of light, in which the arrangement of the glass panels and the choice of furniture were the essential elements for the architects.

The second scheme was set in a Neo-Classical building dating from the early 20th century. The client acquired the whole property and decided to remodel two of the flats to create his private dwelling: a large, bright apartment facing the garden.

The spaces had previously been used as small dwellings and had undergone many modifications over the years. To create the new dwelling, most of the walls were demolished, while the floors, windows and original radiators were conserved. One of the main interventions was the creation of a complex stairwell between the two floors, with glazed openings like those of churches. On the upper floor a major feature is the modern design of the bathroom, with a high bathtub designed by the architects and placed strategically to offer panoramic views of the port of Stockholm.

Photographs: Partrick Engquist - Åke E: Son Lindman

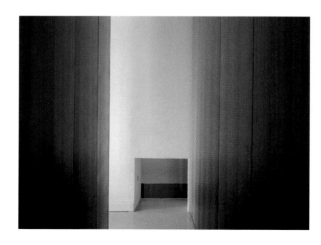

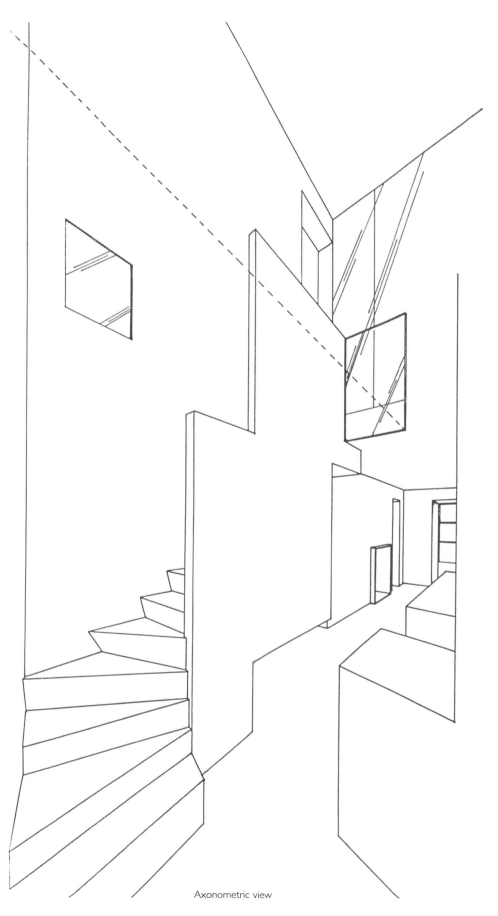

Axonometric view

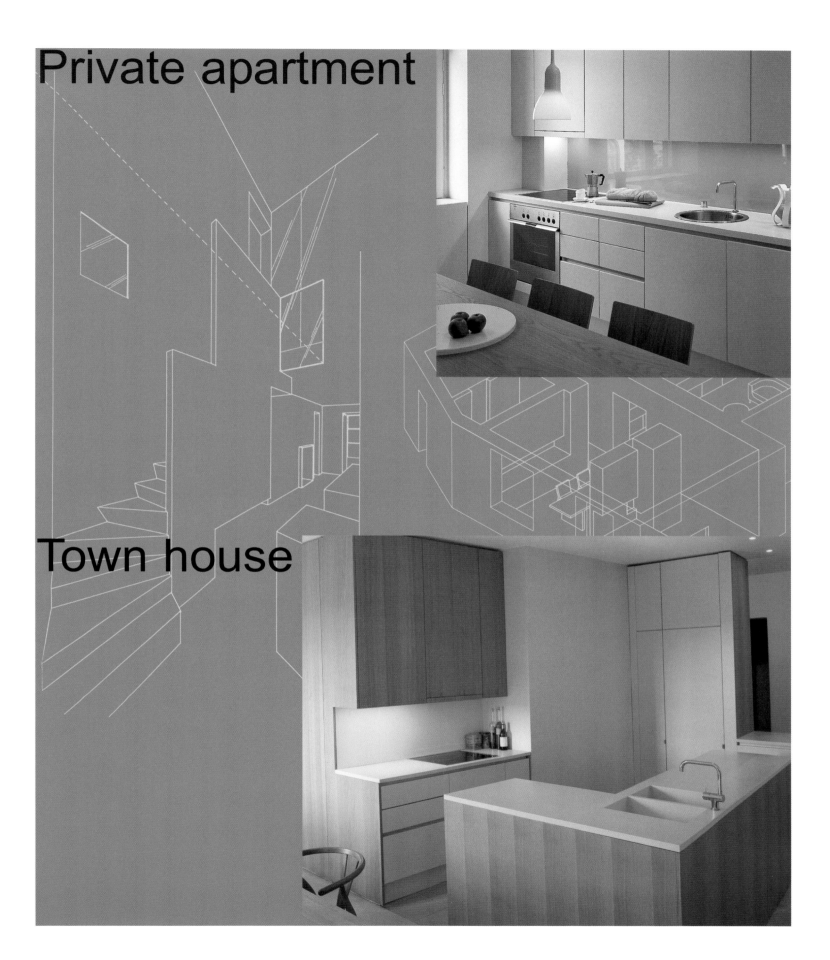

Private apartment

Town house

The dishwasher, refrigerator, freezer and oven are totally integrated behind the doors. Great care was taken with the lighting and the choice of furniture.

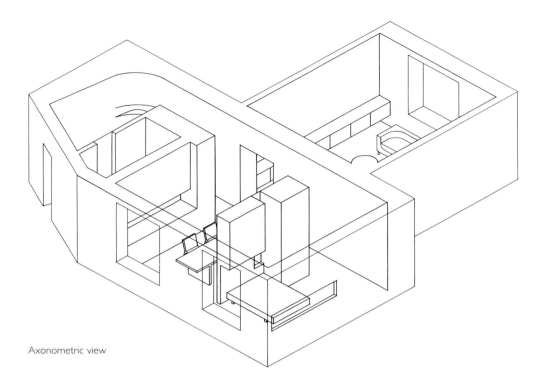

Axonometric view

An essential factor is the vertical and horizontal composition of the openings: a vertical opaque pane in the door communicating the entrance area and the bathroom, a horizontal one between the bathroom and the kitchen, a translucent vertical panel between the dining room and the bedroom, and a mirror at the end of the bedroom wall creating the illusion of a continuous space.

K. A Nordström

An outdoor space is becoming a privilege in large cities. In the photograph on the left, a three-meter-long concrete table was specially designed by the architects for this small oasis of tranquillity.

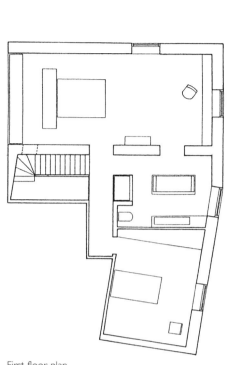

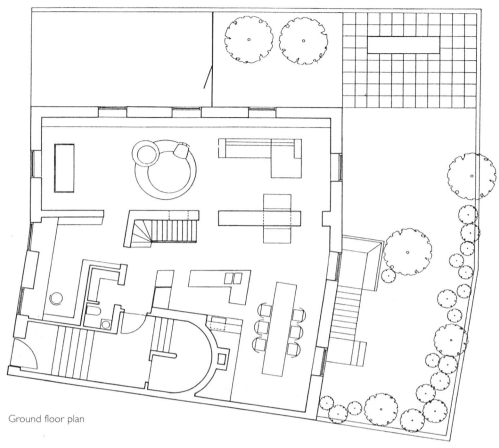

First floor plan

Ground floor plan

The geometry of this project is distinguished by its simplicity and functionalism. The straight lines and the contrast between the different materials highlight the new volumes, giving the whole a modern appearance.

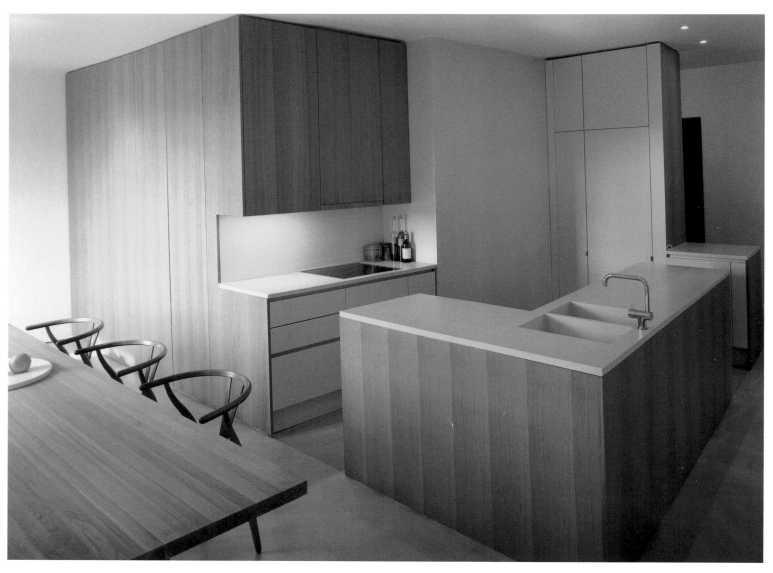

Fausto Colombo
Palazzo Cavagna-Sangiuliani

Pavia, Italy

With its F-Shaped plan, *Palazzo Cavagna-Sangiuliani* in the center of old Pavia is an interesting example of late Quattrocento Pavian architecture (Renaissance architectural design had to be adapted to the spatial constraints of a medieval urban fabric) that also testifies to the stylistic changes of later centuries. Skilful restoration of the almost derelict palazzo to convert it into a home and a notary's office has removed the later additions to reveal the hidden symmetries, rhythmical scansion and frescoes of the original structure. The de-composition and subsequent re-composition of the various parts had made the palazzo a multi-purpose building once again. The restored building is laid out around three courtyards on three floors, each serving a particular function.

The ground floor is devoted entirely to offices. With direct access from the street, the large vaulted hall houses the reception and secretarial office. The hall divides the meeting room from the notary's private office and is the hub of the office complex. The meeting room has walls decorated with Renaissance frescoes of the Lombardy school (the maidens and hunting scenes are unusual in Pavia), a coffered ceiling and an oak and walnut floor bordered with stone. A camber-arched wall with glass in the upper part and sliding leaf doors below separates the meeting room from the waiting area.

The first floor is the day area of perceptively sequenced rooms placed along the internal facade. The wooden ceiling and the stone floor are linked by their geometric design.

The second floor houses the spaces for study and rest. What it loses in distributive clarity, it gains in composition and in the variety of unusual elements. The homogeneity of the treatment of walls and floors and the diffuse luminosity tend to provide visual uniformity. This conversion aims to recover the image of the residential palazzo structured around a courtyard and open to the city, thus contributing to the reorganization of the old center and the requalification of the environment context.

Photographs: Cesare Colombo

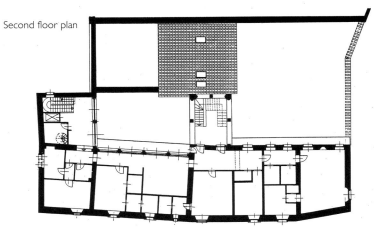

Second floor plan

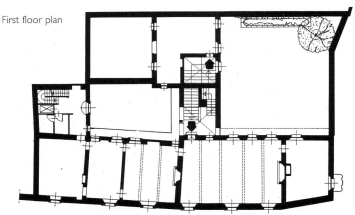

First floor plan

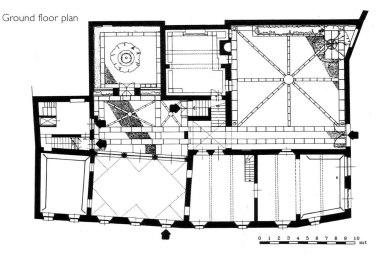

Ground floor plan

0 1 2 3 4 5 6 7 8 9 10 mt

The building is organized spatially through two inner courtyards separated from the body of the building through a third courtyard. These can be accessed directly from the street.

In the second inner courtyard the pavement has been restored. It is built of river pebbles in the Lombardy style, following a geometric plan traced in stone.

Longitudinal section

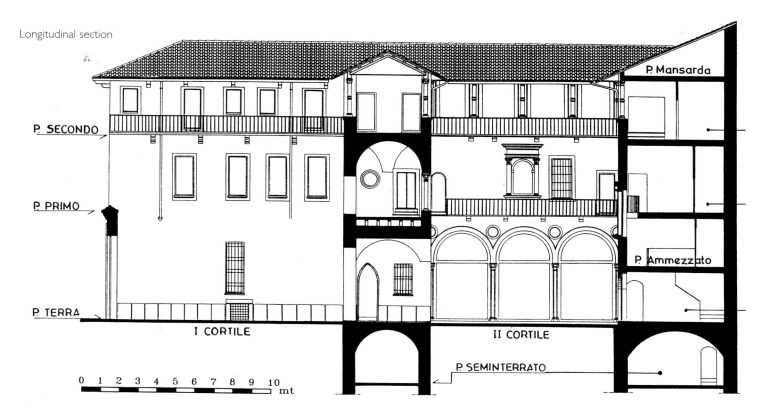

P. SECONDO

P. PRIMO

P. TERRA

I CORTILE

II CORTILE

P. Mansarda

P. Ammezzato

P. SEMINTERRATO

0 1 2 3 4 5 6 7 8 9 10 mt

The upper floor opens onto the inner courtyard through a loggia supported by free-standing stone columns crowned by small capitals. This loggia runs along the whole length of one of the outer walls of the second courtyard.

The restoration of the building revealed the existence of important frescoes of the Bramante school in two of the main rooms: the notary's study and the meeting room.

ARTEC Architekten
Raum Zita Kern

Raasdorf, Austria

Following the needs of the owner, a literature scholar who was fond of the country life, a new and provocative building element was constructed in the old farm of Marchfeld. The fundamental requirement was to create a large and comfortable office for reading and writing, far from the noisy atmosphere of the city. The conversion also required the construction of a bathroom and a toilet and the installation of a complete heating system.

The starting point for the design was the former cowshed, whose roof was in danger of falling in and had to be completely removed. The new roof was prolonged with the incorporation of a staircase located on the exterior, creating an unusual shape that marks the contrast between old and new. The original module was made use of as far as possible, so that the same building served as a basis for a new architectural element. The whole facade of the cowshed is clad in aluminum, creating an experience that remains in the memory of visitors. In the interior, materials such as poplar plywood and aluminum break away from the rural atmosphere and provide a cosmopolitan and welcoming air.

The bathroom is located in the main building and is illuminated by a flat skylight. On it, the rainwater can collect up to a depth of two centimetres, thus creating special effects of shades.

The new office is located on the first floor, a space that is calm and distant from its surroundings and conducive to the full force of the intellect. This study opens onto two terraces through sliding doors that extend the room even more. The location of the terraces helps to illuminate the interior of the dwelling and makes a decisive contribution to the peculiar form of the scheme.

Photographs: Margherita Spiluttini

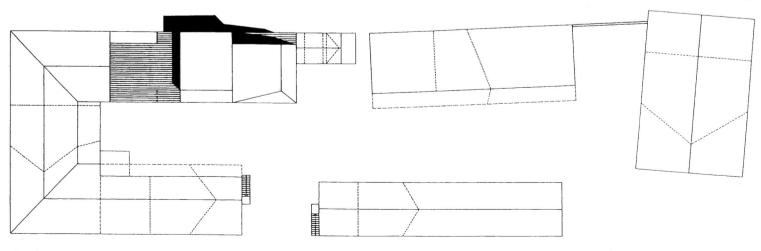

Site plan.

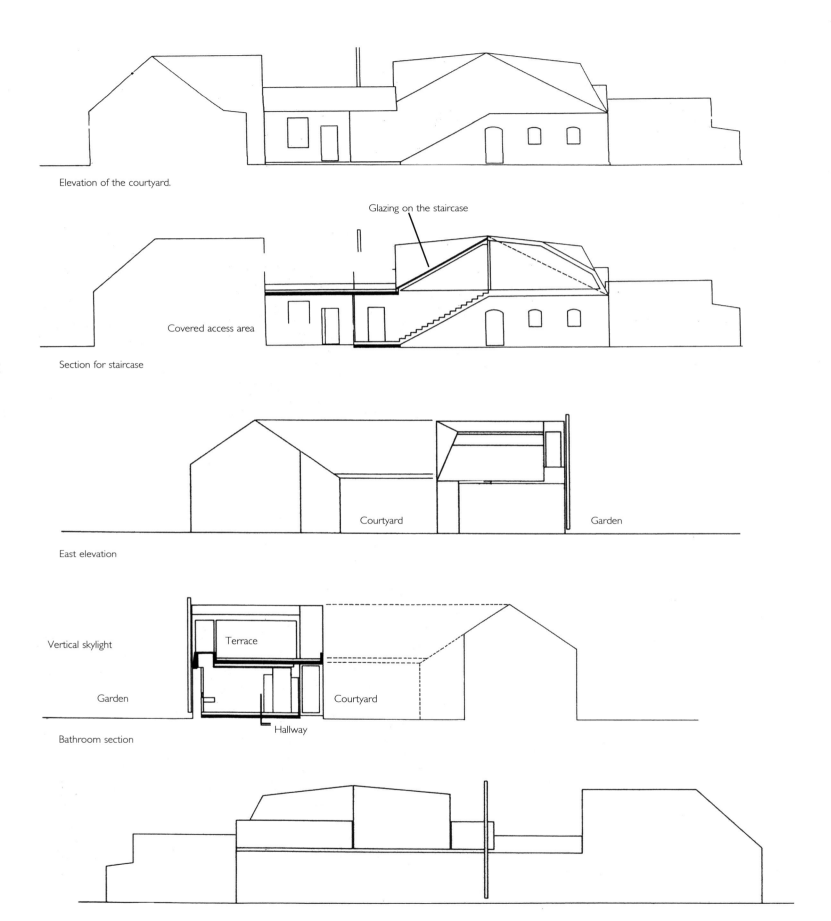

Elevation of the courtyard.

Glazing on the staircase

Covered access area

Section for staircase

East elevation

Courtyard

Garden

Vertical skylight

Terrace

Garden

Courtyard

Hallway

Bathroom section

North elevation

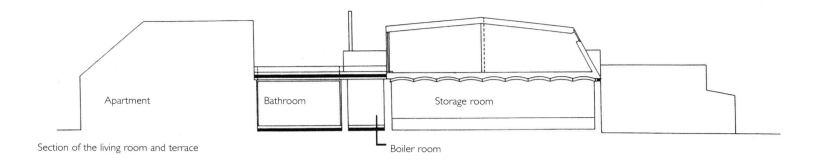

Apartment   Bathroom   Storage room

Section of the living room and terrace   Boiler room

The opposition between the construction materials of the old building and those used for the new room creates a special effect by merging the urban and rural atmospheres.

The impact achieved by incorporating aluminum into this old agricultural building helps to integrate the rest of the buildings in this farm complex.

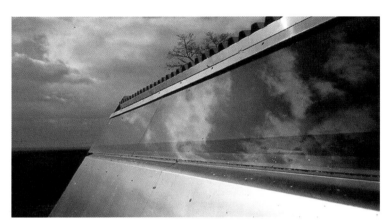

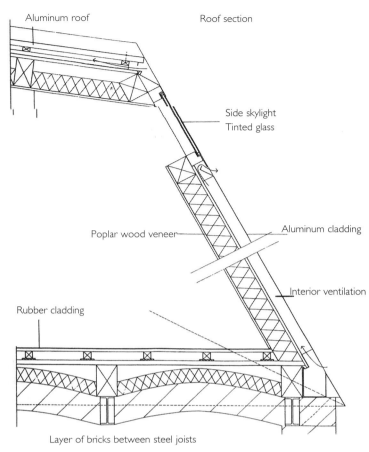

Roof section

Aluminum roof

Side skylight
Tinted glass

Poplar wood veneer

Aluminum cladding

Interior ventilation

Rubber cladding

Layer of bricks between steel joists

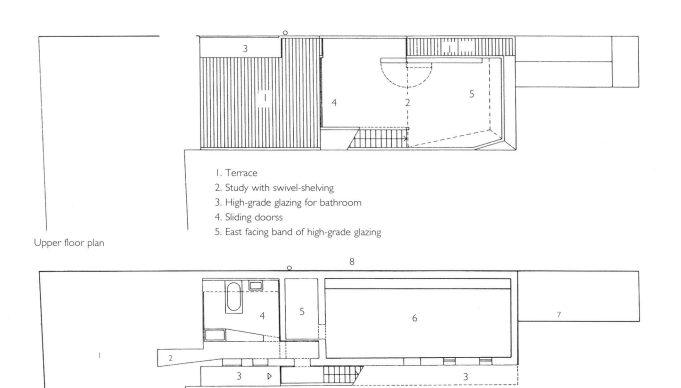

Upper floor plan

1. Terrace
2. Study with swivel-shelving
3. High-grade glazing for bathroom
4. Sliding doorss
5. East facing band of high-grade glazing

Ground floor plan

1. Apartment building
2. Hallway
3. Covered area
4. Bathroom with high-level glazing
5. Boiler room
6. Storage room
7. Chicken coop
8. Garden
9. Courtyard

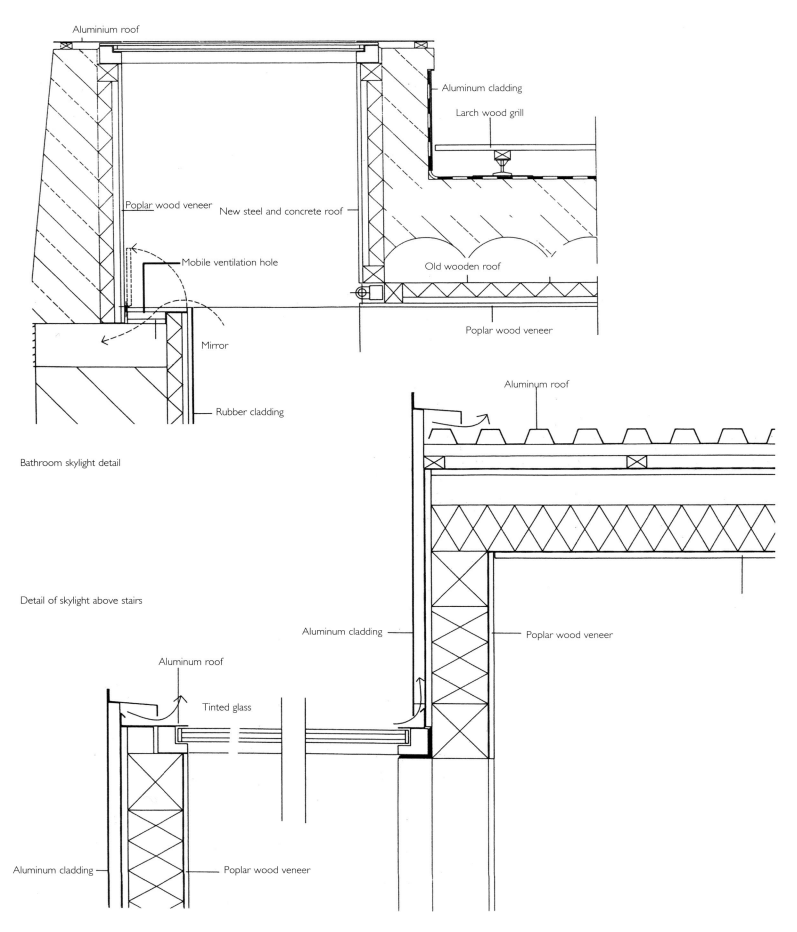

Aluminium roof

Aluminum cladding

Larch wood grill

Poplar wood veneer   New steel and concrete roof

Mobile ventilation hole

Old wooden roof

Poplar wood veneer

Mirror

Rubber cladding

Bathroom skylight detail

Aluminum roof

Detail of skylight above stairs

Aluminum cladding   Poplar wood veneer

Aluminum roof

Tinted glass

Aluminum cladding   Poplar wood veneer

124

Brightness and simple forms were key elements in defining the interior spaces of this dwelling. This is most clearly appreciated in the color and smooth textures of the staircase and bathroom.

Non Kitch Group bvba
Architecture and lifestyle

Koksijde, Belgium

Transforming an old canning factory in Bruges into an impressive loft dwelling was a great challenge with endless attractive possibilities for the designers. One of the most significant features of this scheme by architect Linda Arschoot and designer William Sweetlove, the creators of the Non Kitch Group, was the remodelled roof. It was formed by a lattice structure with a dog-tooth profile supporting a conventional roof. They decided to replace the north sides of each of the parallel roofs with a glazed surface. These skylights greatly increase the natural lighting in the whole dwelling, as in many museums or art galleries. Due to the considerable height of the building (6 meters), this intervention also meant that the interior was almost converted into an outside piazza. A large, full-height room open to the exterior occupies the center of the space and is surrounded by a mezzanine that houses the kitchen, dining room, bar and television room. Under this mezzanine, three steps below the level of the living room, are the billiards room, bedroom, dressing room, gym and the bathroom that opens directly onto the small garden. The covered pool is located on one side of this exterior space, with an elegant strip of mosaic tiles. An outdoor area also provides better views and enhances the dimensions of the space.

The conservation of the industrial aspect of the building is shown through the use of metal doors, heating pipes, a separate kitchen, the galvanized iron staircase and the view of the old factory chimney through the parallel skylights of the roof. In opposition to the asceticism of minimalist interiors, the Non Kitch Group feel themselves to be the heirs of the humor and colorist aesthetics of the Memphis group. One of the premises of this scheme was to generate an appropriate space for viewing the works of art in the private collection of the owners. The furniture is a forceful presence in this dwelling. Designed by Ettore Sottsass, Philippe Starck, Boris Spiek, Jean Nouvel, Norman Foster and the architects themselves, it seems to be made to measure for this spacious loft.

Photographs: Jan Verlinde

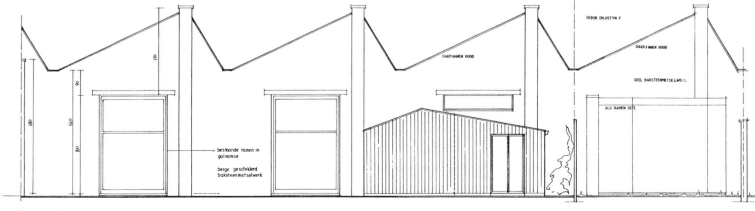

Elevation A

The conservation of the industrial aspect of the building is shown through the use of metal doors, heating pipes, a separate kitchen, the galvanized iron staircase and the view of the old factory chimney through the parallel skylights of the roof.

Elevation B

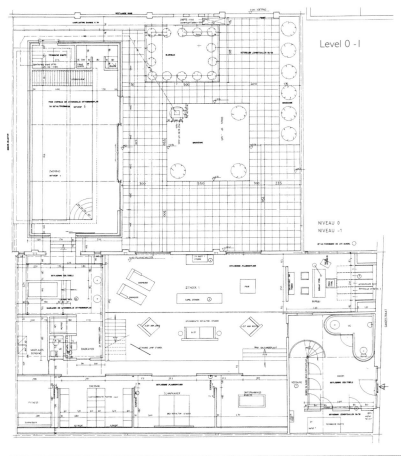

Level 0 -1

NIVEAU 0
NIVEAU -1

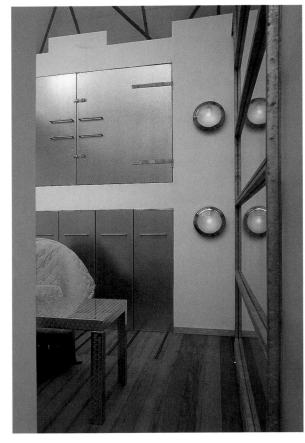

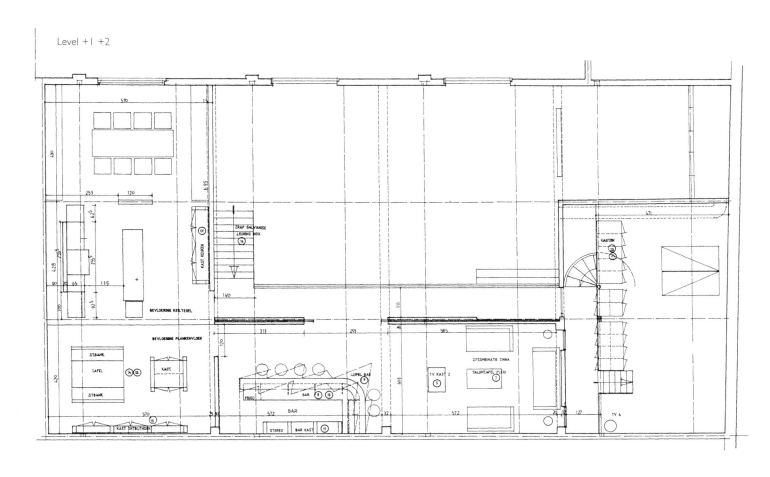

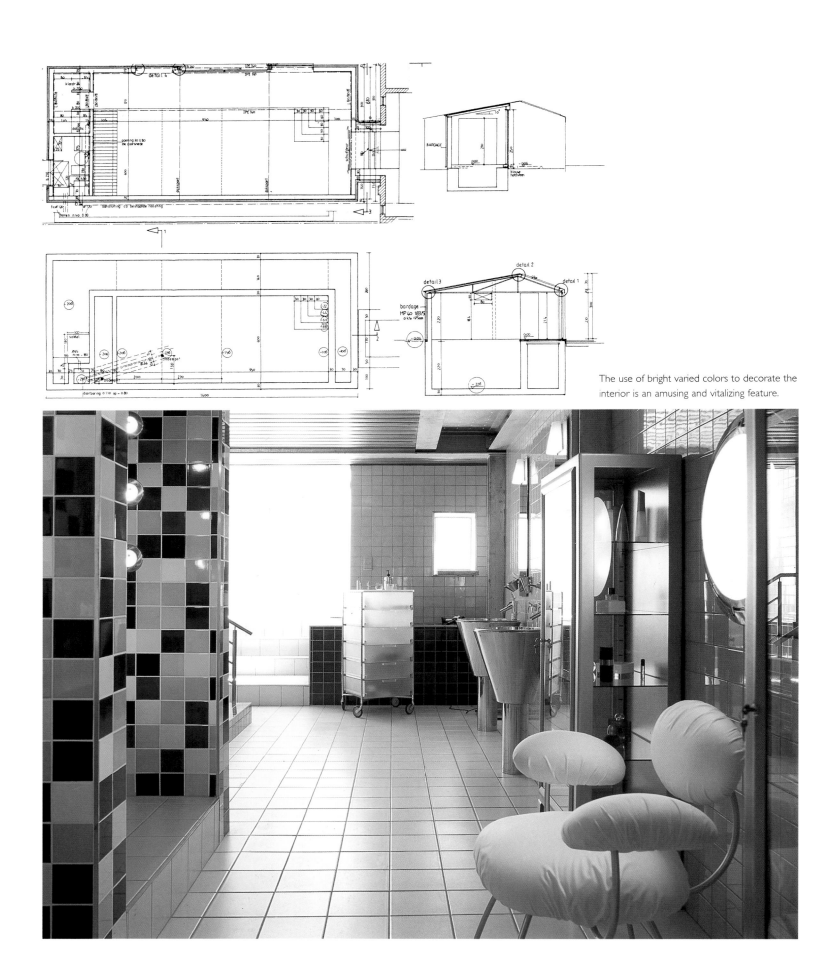

The use of bright varied colors to decorate the interior is an amusing and vitalizing feature.

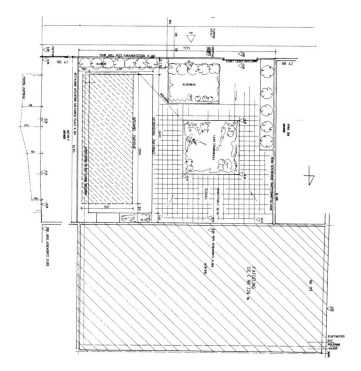

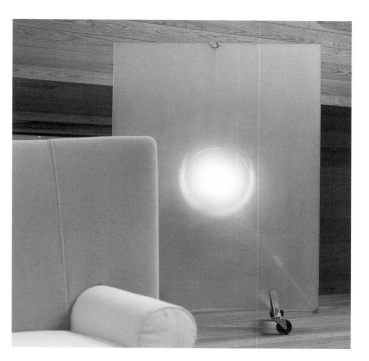

The metal elements used throughout the loft contribute an industrial air that recalls the former use of the building. The central location of the kitchen and the simple forms are a clear example of the emotions and contrasts sought by the Non Kitch Group.

Kar-Hwa Ho
Apartment in New York

New York, USA

The anonymity and light-starved north-facing orientation of one of the many lofts in New York's Chelsea district have been more than remedied in this well considered response to the needs of the client, a bachelor employed in the financial sector. His first requirement —greater unity and definition in the existing layout— is fulfilled by a spatial narrative that creates a marked distinction between the spaces for formal dining and gatherings in the living area, and the tranquillity and quiet of the bedrooms. To accentuate the clean, simple geometry of the space, moldings, baseboards and trim have been removed and the walls and columns realigned and reproportioned. Removing the suspended ceiling in the living area to expose the continuous structural vaults has added an almost frivolous touch to the design.

The living area is a large single space whose functional divisions are marked by carefully chosen commercial and custom furnishings.

The bedroom is dominated by a custom maple platform bed with blanket and pillow storage in its headboard. Two recessed bedside tables with backlit sandblasted glass sides and adjustable glass shelves and reading lamps, all custom designed by the architect. The sunshades accentuate the simplicity of the white geometrical space. The existing oak floor has been stained a darker shade.

Photographs: Björg Photography

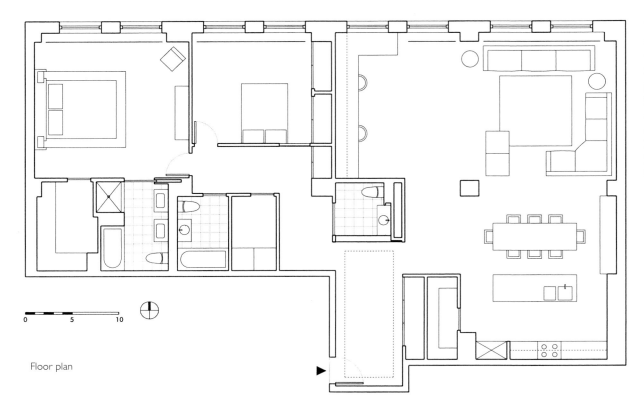

The kitchen has been custom-designed. The maple credenza with nesting mobile maple units below features frosted glass front and back panels. Sensuous, tactile textures —warm woods, translucent or sandblasted glass, stainless steel— have been used for the furnishings to counterpoint the simplicity of the furniture and spaces.

Floor plan

0   5   10

Jean-Paul Bonnemaison
House in Lubéron

Lubéron, France

The building is located strategically beside the church of a small village in Haute Provence, with good views of the street and the adjoining fields. The dwelling was built on the ruins of an old oil mill with the intention of preserving the memory of what was formerly one of the main sources of wealth in the area.

It fits perfectly into the building codes of this village, as it conserves several external walls and follows a program based on the urban volumetrics that amplifies the perspectives of the main street, thus respecting the style of the neighboring buildings and the dominance of the church. The small, sharply sloping plot is fully occupied by abundant terraces and gardens that are crossed by a path that leads to an existing swimming pool.

The facades are clearly differentiated, and the public facade faces the town with five stone steps that emphasize the main entrance. The circular windows in the wall provide privacy and give the residents splendid views of the church steeple and the castle. This facade has a stone structure and has been intensified architecturally by means of jalousie windows that offer views of the town whilst protecting the interior from excessive sunlight. The other facade, which faces the fields, is private and totally glazed. Its design faithfully represents the changes of a society: new materials and construction systems combined with respect for nature.

The project is broken down horizontally into two groups, one containing the services and the guest area, and the other containing the main room of the house. Vertically, this main group consists of four levels, the last one with a bedroom, bathroom and terrace. The living room occupies three levels, with terraces that ensure spatial continuity with the sloping garden. A completely transparent metal staircase connects the different levels. The incorporation of this element on the glazed facade combines with the environment and allows the inhabitants to enjoy a different room, sitting in it as if it were a theater.

The interior design is governed by the elegant and simple requirements of the clients, who are fascinated by Cistercian art, and includes hints of minimalism. The interior walls were painted white to capture the natural light of Provence and to highlight the collection of sketches that decorate the house. The light-colored stone, the bluish gray of the structure and the beige of the cement areas fit into the general coloring of the town while giving the house a special character.

Photographs: Leonard de Selva

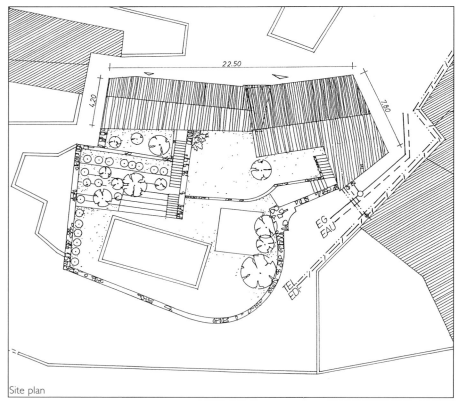

Site plan

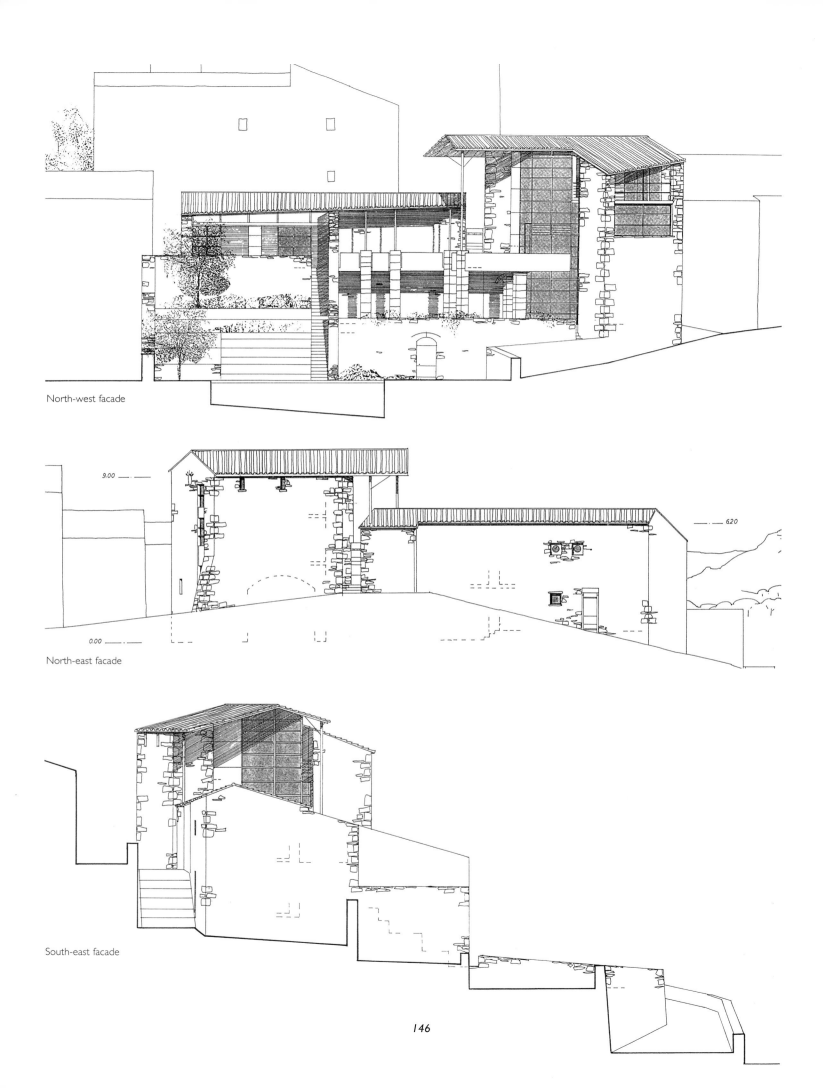

North-west facade

9.00

0.00

6.20

North-east facade

South-east facade

146

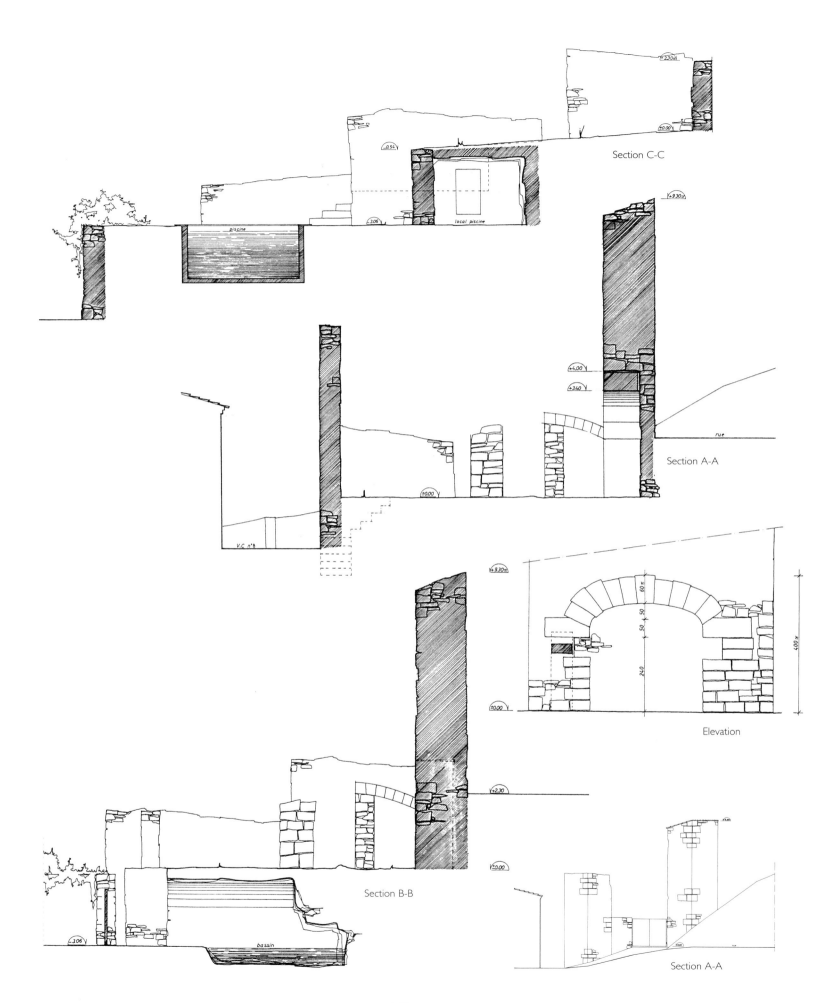

Section C-C

Section A-A

Elevation

Section B-B

Section A-A

147

The broken form of the staircase provides a continuous solution to the great difference in level between the floors of the dwelling. Its situation in front of the window converts it into a kind of a tier from which one can contemplate the landscape and the interior space.

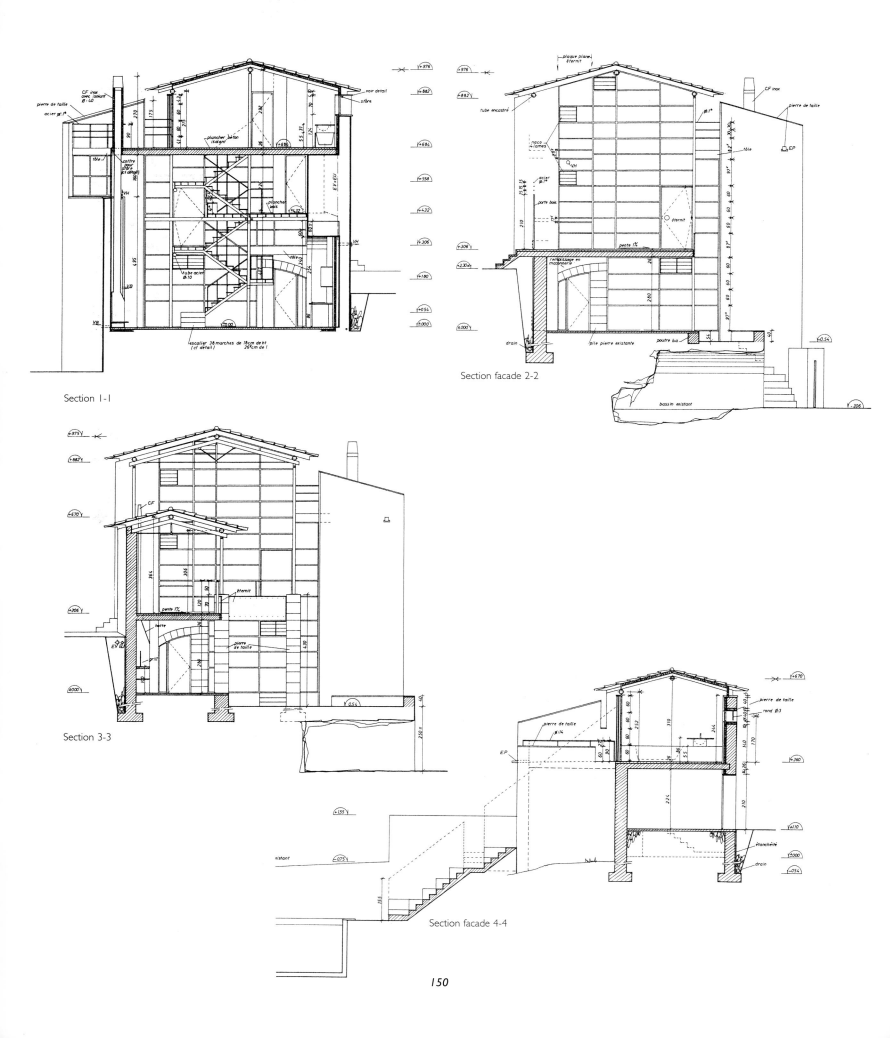

Section 1-1

Section facade 2-2

Section 3-3

Section facade 4-4

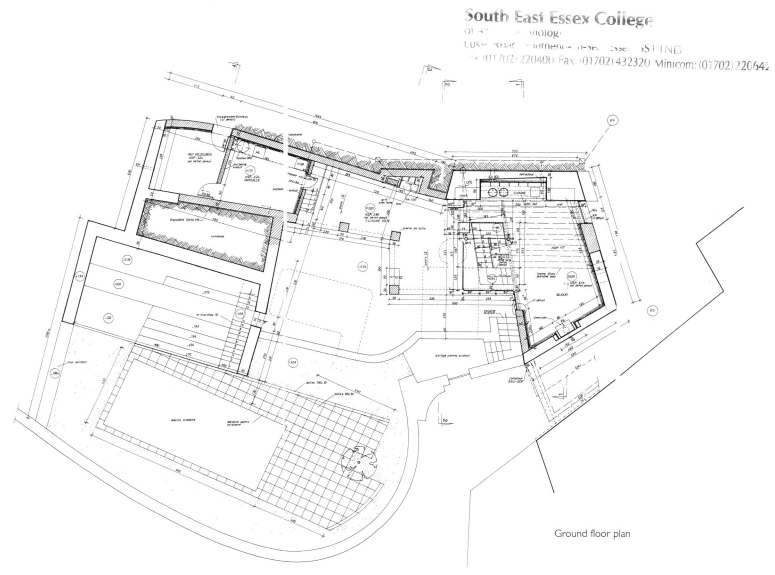

Ground floor plan

First floor plan

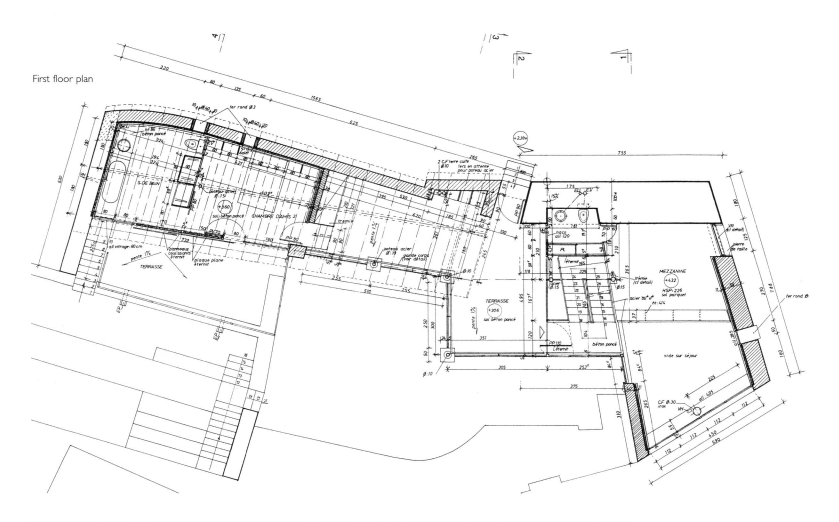

The compositional pattern of the glass on the facade is emphasized in the interior by the mirrors in the bathroom.

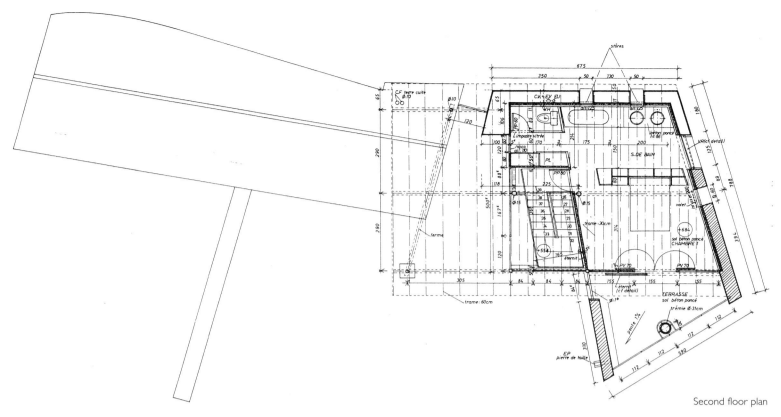

Second floor plan

153

Fernando Távora
House in Pardelhas

Pardelhas, Portugal

This country house is located in a mountainous area near Vila Nova de Cerveira, in northern Portugal. It is a farm building with spaces of small dimensions that forms part of a set of three houses with identical typologies, each one defined by a closed exterior space. The three different nuclei were practically in ruins and their structure was hardly supported by the wide granite walls.

The houses establish relationships of vicinity so that different exterior spaces enhance each other and give form to the whole, with enveloping walls and corridors.

The scheme seeks to take advantage of the habitability of the existing structure, adapting it to a new use and recovering the traditional construction process of tiled roofs with wooden beams that provides a better reading of the existing structure. The new layout is freed from the upper space to give way to the main room, which is in direct contact with the kitchen, and to a second room that was entirely rebuilt in wood. The private area of the house, containing the bedrooms and bathrooms, is located on the lower floor in direct contact with the exterior courtyard. The canopy of the entrance passage is made of wood, supported by existing stone platforms, establishing a continuity with the exterior railing and with the main room. The house and the annex are joined by a corridor, defining a more private and independent space.

The house itself follows the same logic of intervention, using the walls to contain its new spaces, which form an independent section that is self-sufficient from the main house, with bedroom, living room, kitchen and bathroom.

Photographs: Luis Ferreira Alves

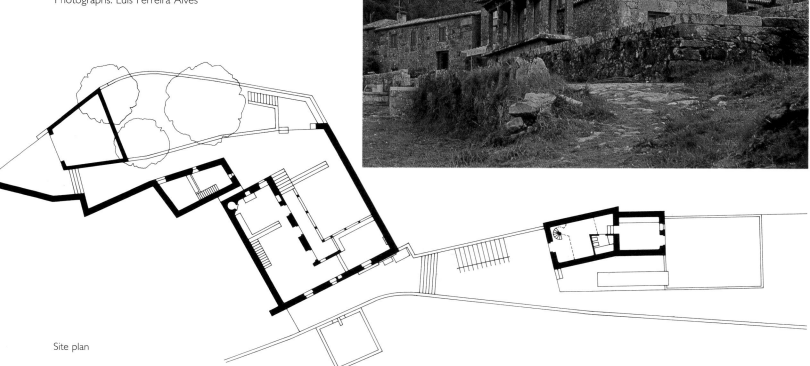

Site plan

The rural character of this dwelling and its environment disappears almost completely in the interior. The combination of new materials helps to emphasize the natural lighting, creating an unexpected feeling of comfort in a house built of granite.

156

Julian Cowie Architects
Fleetwood Place

London, UK

For passers-by, Fleetwood school in Stoke Newington may seem a typical 1880s Victorian institutional building. However, Julian Cowie Architects and London Wharf developers have changed its interior image completely, successfully converting an undervalued building into deluxe apartments.

In 1917, two large additional blocks were inserted in the angles formed by the main wings of the school. The new floor levels were never aligned and the internal circulation conserves a curious character full of differences. Before one goes through the glazed door, the first impression of the building is one of warmth and comfort. The sandblasted brick walls, the upholstered seats on the landing, and the ash wood doors are small details that give the sensation of great care and elegance in the aesthetic design. Each of the thirteen floors of the building is different. They all occupy some of the classroom spaces and they share common elements: a double-height space, an inserted kitchen, a central bathroom and a mezzanine (or two) with a bedroom above the service nucleus.

The two flats presented here give an idea of the different inventive transformations that were carried out in these properties.

The first one, located on the upper floor, is occupied by a photographer and has an extraordinary wooden framework that serves as a support for the roof. On this occasion there are two mezzanines which are accessed by means of two spiral staircases of galvanized steel. While one houses the bedroom, the other small one in the center is used by the owner as a retreat.. He has installed a study below it, partly enclosed by capacious storage walls wich divide the floor space and provide a discrete dining area.

In the second, a music lover occupies a mostly rectangular space in which it was decided to continue the mezzanine along the interior wall in order to provide an additional, fully equipped bedroom. The area of the original mezzanine houses a bedroom and a small corner that is used as an office. Above all, the apartments were designed to be flexible.

Photographs: Peter Cook / View

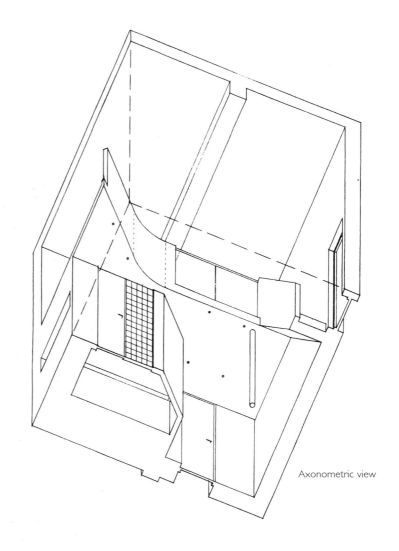

Axonometric view

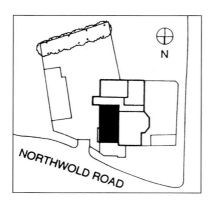

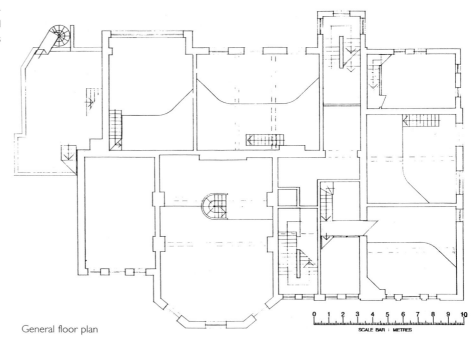

General floor plan

0 1 2 3 4 5 6 7 8 9 10
SCALE BAR : METRES

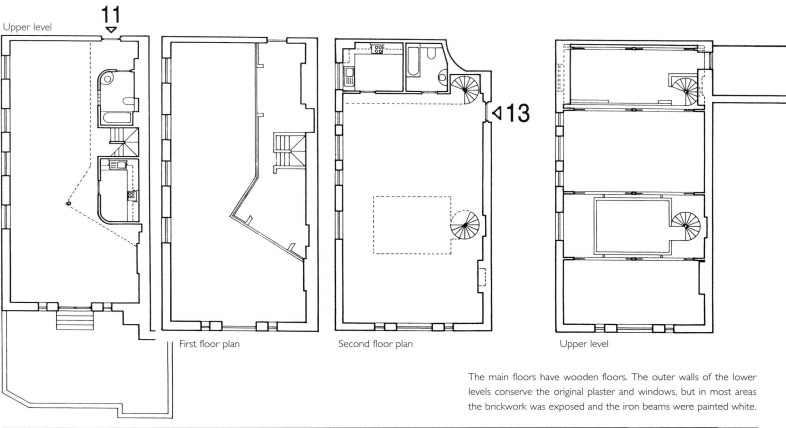

Upper level

First floor plan   Second floor plan   Upper level

The main floors have wooden floors. The outer walls of the lower levels conserve the original plaster and windows, but in most areas the brickwork was exposed and the iron beams were painted white.

Julia B. Bolles & Peter L. Wilson
Haus Dub

Münster, Germany

This small addition to a 1960's Modernist atrium house respects the language of the object in which is found.

The team of architects Julia Bolles and Peter Wilson have made a careful and exquisite rehabilitation, based, as they declare, in the "fascination for clarity, optimism and simple geometries of the last days of functionalism".

The structure of the original house is transcended through the insertion of a new vertical element, a volume covered by intense blue brick that looks to the internal court. This foreign object, that emphasises and puts energy into the geometry of the complex, breaks through the artificial horizon of the existing flat roof.

Necessitated by new use requirements (a larger living space, a small studio) the new additions are reduced to five discrete elements: the blue glazed brick wall, the zinc wall, the sun louvers (a new horizontal factor), the internal swing wall and, as a nexus for the whole composition, the central fireplace.

Photographs: Christian Richters

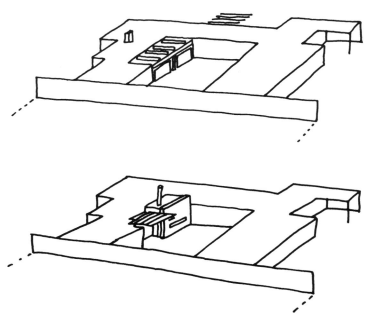

Sketches before and after the intervention

The project aims to solve the problems of space of the existing building by providing sufficient floor area to extend the living-room and create a small studio.

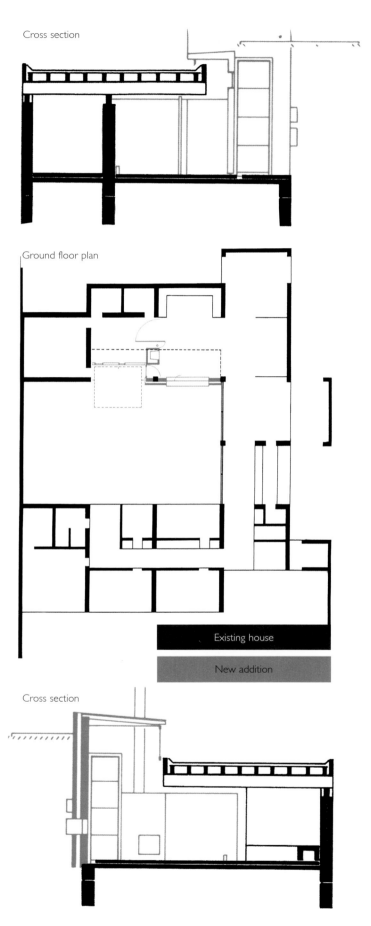

Cross section

Ground floor plan

Existing house

New addition

Cross section

South elevation   North elevation

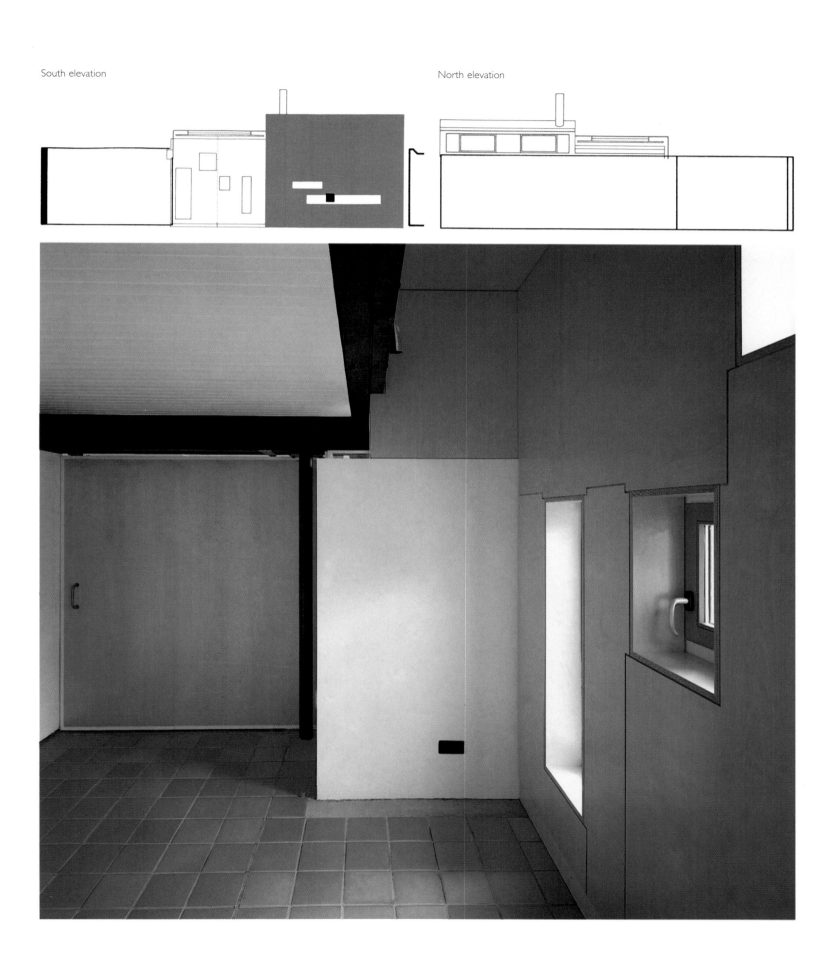

Jahn Associates Architects
Grant House

Sidney, Australia

The Grant House is located in the back streets of inner city Sydney, where rows of terrace houses are separated by small-scale industrial warehouses. The site was originally a timber yard and the original exterior brick walls have been retained to face the street and act as an apron to the layers of timber and steel that make up the new facade. Two of the Oregon pine trusses from the original building have been reused over the first floor living area.

Entry is through the outer brick skin and is marked simply by a galvanized steel lintel plate. Through this portal, the threshold space between the street and the interior allows contemplation of the sanctum within.

The idea of the home as a sanctuary in the city is central to the design, defining the organization of the spaces within the building and their materiality. The house is stacked to the south, enabling a ground-level, north-facing courtyard to emerge. The courtyard allows for natural day lighting of the interior, controlled by operable aluminum louvers on the ground floor to screen the lower bedrooms. Situated within this tranquil and contemplative space is the timber-clad studio, designed as a workspace and meditation room. It is placed to take advantage of the courtyard's water feature as well as providing a visual and physical link with the street entry.

The interior spaces are calm and protective, wrapping around the courtyard, and designed to accommodate an extensive art collection, as well as its future expansion.

The interior play of spatial relationships and materials in conjunction with the folded planes of the exterior, which wrap the surface of the building through its successive skins, unite to both embrace the life of the city and shun it. In addition, the simplicity of the new volume brings a new dimension to the street and encourages interaction through the natural aging of the materials, the original brick shell acting as the catalyst for an inventive and human response to the experience of living in the city.

Photographs: Brett Boardman and Graham Jahn

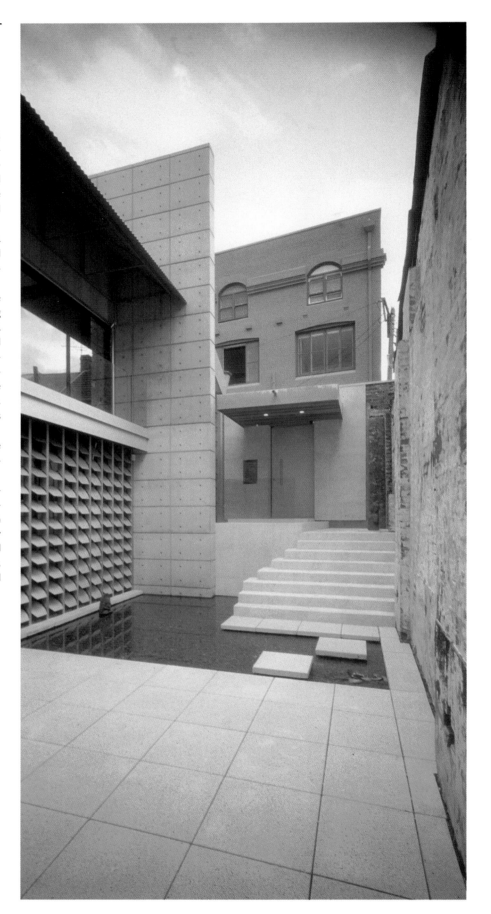

Exploded axonometric view

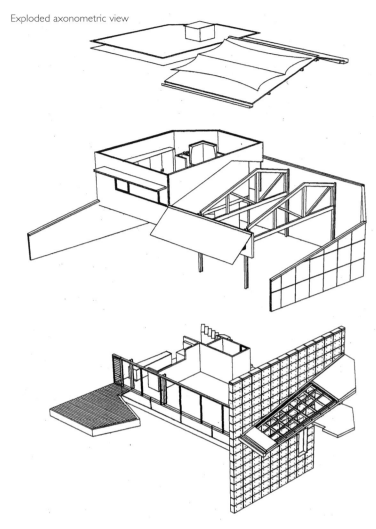

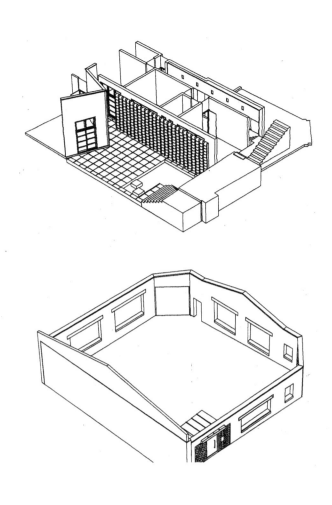

The house is stacked to the south, enabling a ground level, north-facing courtyard to emerge. The courtyard allows for natural day lighting of the interior, controlled by operable aluminum louvers on the ground floor to screen the lower bedrooms.

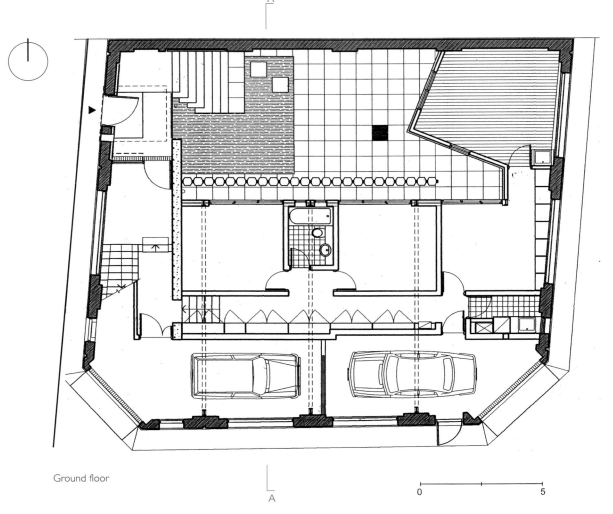

Ground floor

0   5

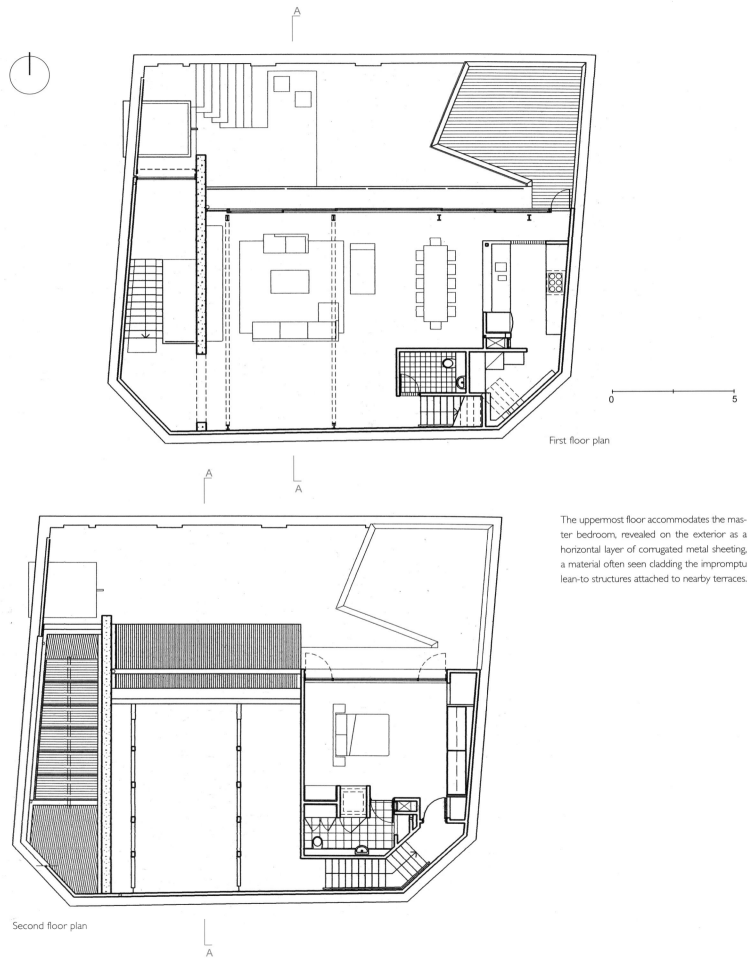

A

First floor plan

0   5

A

A

The uppermost floor accommodates the master bedroom, revealed on the exterior as a horizontal layer of corrugated metal sheeting, a material often seen cladding the impromptu lean-to structures attached to nearby terraces.

Second floor plan

A

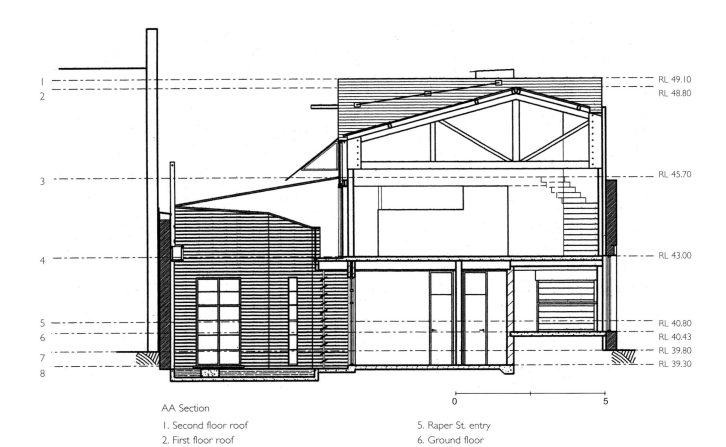

AA Section

1. Second floor roof
2. First floor roof
3. Second floor master bedroom
4. First floor living

5. Raper St. entry
6. Ground floor
7. Studio floor
8. Existing ground floor

RL 49.10
RL 48.80
RL 45.70
RL 43.00
RL 40.80
RL 40.43
RL 39.80
RL 39.30

Kalhöfer & Korschildgen
Holiday House in Normandy

Normandy, France

The old Norman farmhouse was in an extremely rundown condition before the conversion. The aim of the design was to let the holiday house appear as an original building rather than a museum-piece. The most urgent building measures for the conversion of the building were the reconstruction of the existing structure and the fitting out of the kitchen and bathroom. Matching the often collage-like structure of development in the nearby environment, the concept provides for two distinct parts by complementing the historical building with a separate modern building. The layout, light, material and color should provide the inhabitant with a different living experience in the new building and in the restored old building.

The existing building was reconstructed removing the defective elements and using any old materials that could be conserved. The oak doors, wooden floors, natural stone walls and chimneys were reconstructed by the architects according to traditional regional details.

The new building concentrates the necessary technical facilities of a house at a few points. A steel framework serves as a supporting grid for the sanitary fittings and a kind of picture plane to which the coloured surfaces of the finishings are fixed. Flowing transitions of the structure from inside to outside help to create a holiday home that can be used in different ways, depending on the season. The boundaries between inner and outer space are translucent and fluid thanks to the generous use of glass, which is specially striking during the lighting of the individual functional units at night.

Photographs: Rolf Brunsendorf / Jörg Zimmermann

Cross-section

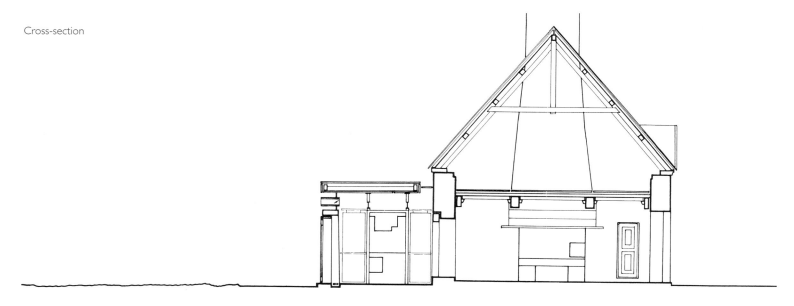

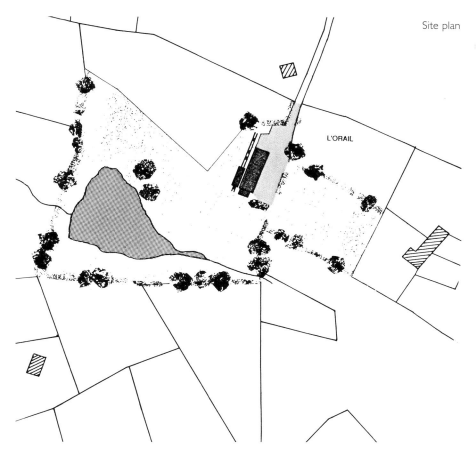

L'ORAIL

South elevation

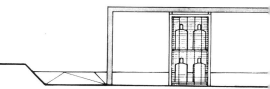

On the opposite page, a view of the east facade, whose appearance has been left practically intact because most of the work was done on the other facades. Below, the south facade before the restoration was carried out.

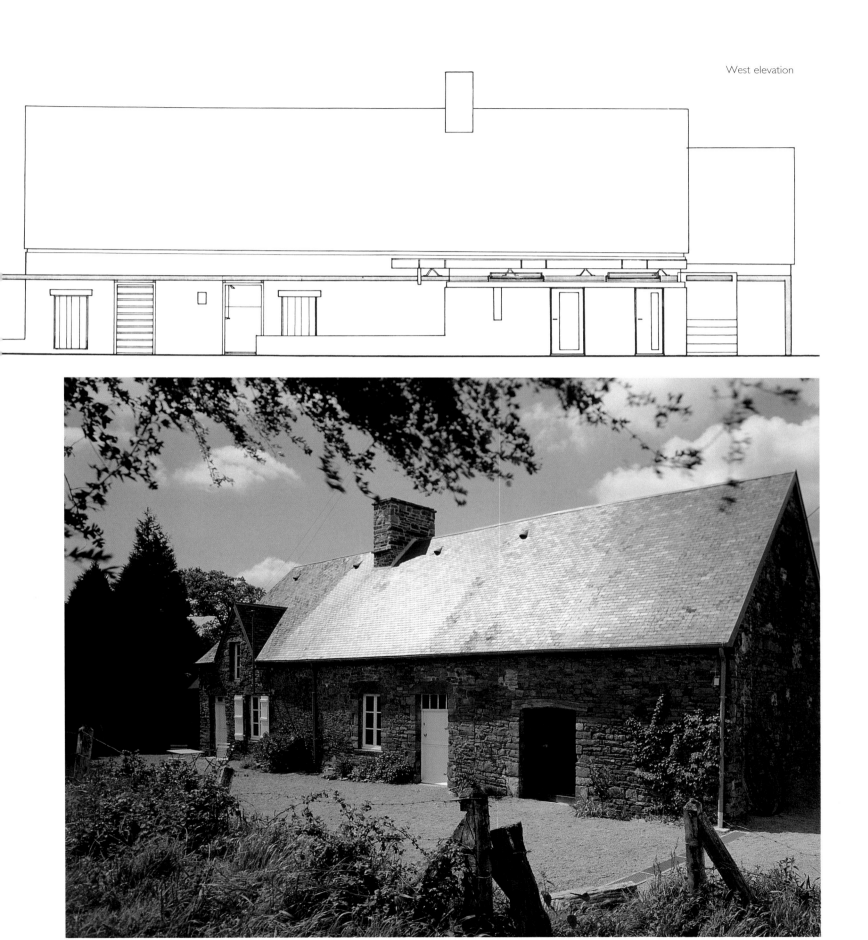

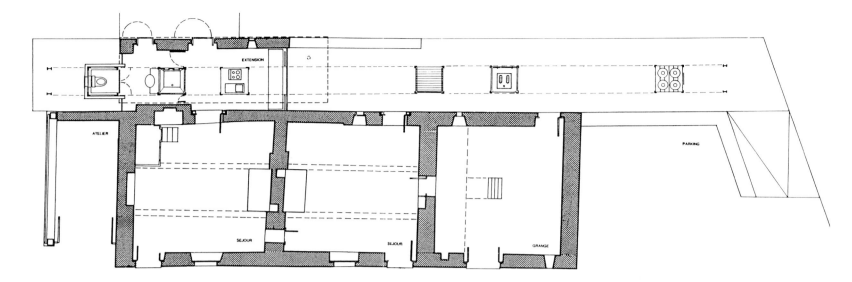

Ground floor plan

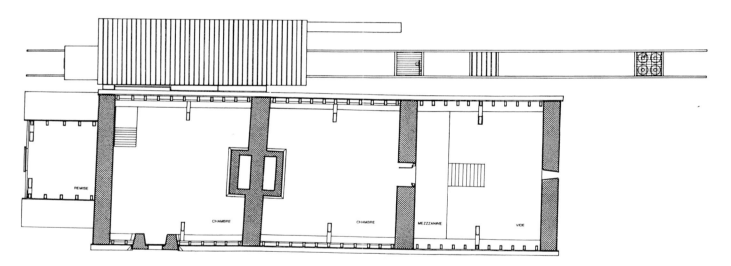

First floor plan

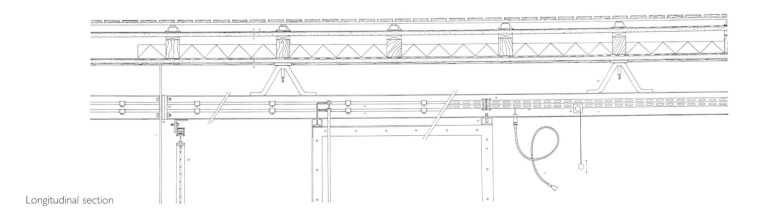

Longitudinal section

The rehabilitation carried out in this building seeks to maintain the original architectural elements and to reconstruct the defective parts using traditional materials.
The annex to the original building is clearly differentiated thanks to its form, material and colors. This extension houses all the necessary services for making the dwelling more comfortable.

Maurice & Enrico Cerasi
Casa Villazzi

Milanino, Italy

Villazzi House is located near Milan in one of the area's most important garden cities. Due to its designation as a protected area, an analysis of the site was undertaken before planning the design. Rather than imitating the preexisting architectural elements of this garden city, the architects chose to reinterpret them, elaborating on a language that respects the character of this historic area.

The house's main body had to be adapted to the structure of a residence built in the 1950s. This articulation is seen in both the facades and the various levels. Unification of volumes and treatment of finishes between the new and old structures was not attempted. Light gray cement and marble powder plaster are set against cement plaster in yellow quartz paint - the smooth surface treatment of the former contrasting with the horizontal grooves of the latter.

Built in three years, the house has six levels and a surface area of more than 4305 ft^2. The conservation of the corridor and wooden stairway in the center of the house prevented the creation of an interior perspective from the street to the garden and necessitated a more traditional interior distribution throughout the house. Access is gained through an entrance courtyard, which is set just below street level and covered by a pergola. The lime trees along the street tastefully accentuate the elegant neoclassical facade.

The formal result has recourse to the languages of the classical past with references to Hellenic architecture, and recalls such masters as Palladio or Schinkel, nullifying the rigor imposed by the original foundation.

Photographs : Andrea Martiradonna & Cerasi Studio

Details and finishes have been treated differently between the more public street-facing portion and the rear facade, which is somewhat plainer and more secluded.

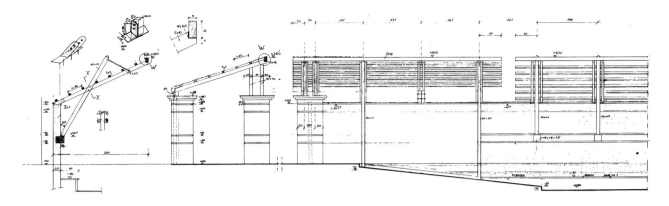

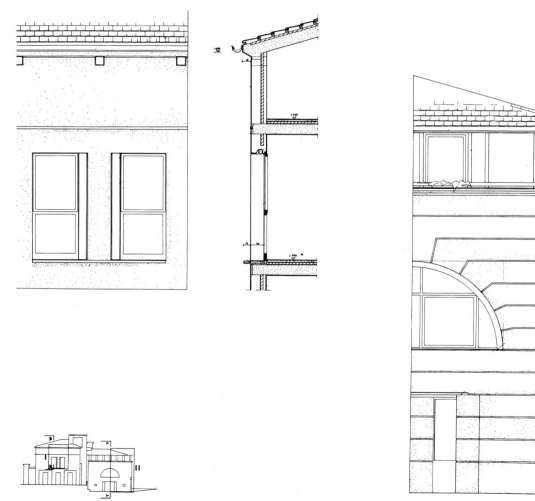

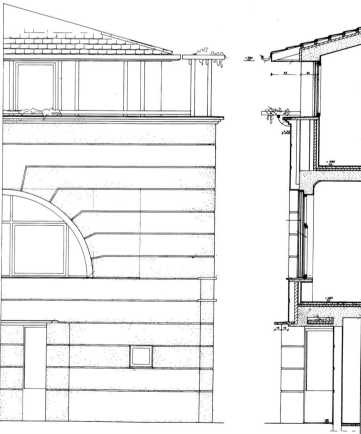

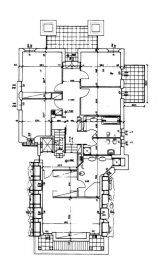

First floor plan

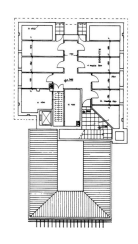

Attic plan

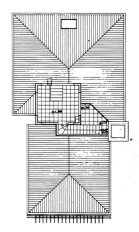

Roof plan

Basement floor plan

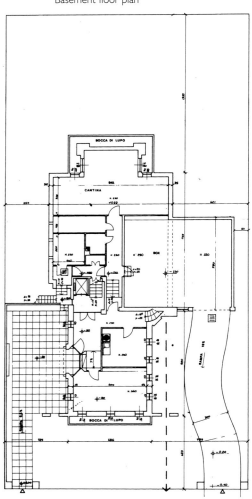

Ground floor plan

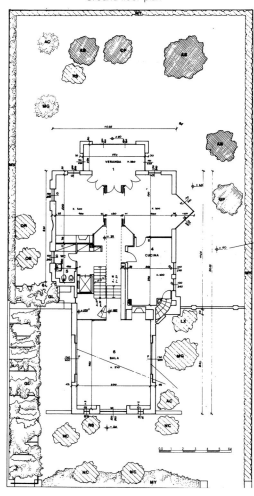

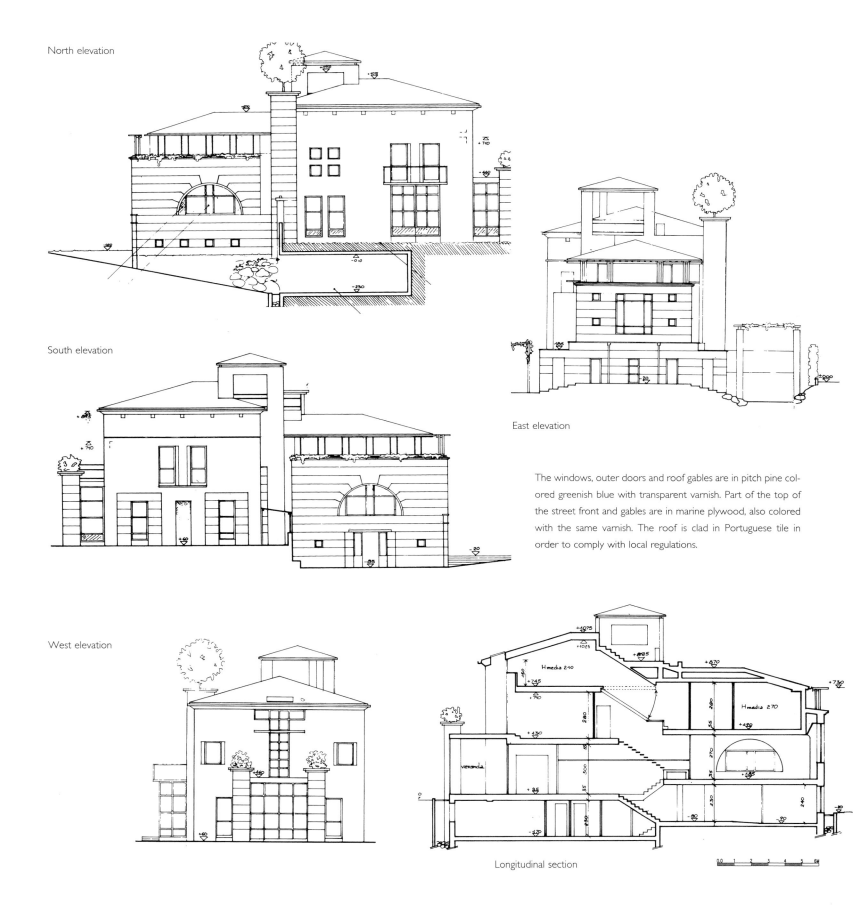

North elevation

South elevation

East elevation

West elevation

The windows, outer doors and roof gables are in pitch pine colored greenish blue with transparent varnish. Part of the top of the street front and gables are in marine plywood, also colored with the same varnish. The roof is clad in Portuguese tile in order to comply with local regulations.

Longitudinal section

Paul Robbrecht & Hilde Daem
The Mys House

Oudenaarde, Belgium

This house, originally built in the eighteenth-century in a provincial town near Ghent, has been gradually transformed. It stands on a narrow plot of land on the banks of the river De Scheide at Oudenaarde. To the rear is a lush walled garden and terrace overlooked by a gabled extension and a glass-house. On the street side, a new glass and steel loggia built to replace the gate to the old coach house has been made into the main entrance to the house. It is the external intimation of the changes within; but otherwise, the handsome facade remains intact.

The original building, with later additions, consisted of a sequence of interconnecting rooms stretching back from the street and linked on the ground floor by the glass-house. A cone open to the sky and traversed by a narrow metal bridge penetrates the central part of the house so that light pouring down illuminates the library on the first floor. Open space for the children was created by raising the roof and making a huge attic playroom. On the ground floor, the existing glasshouse was retained and carefully restored, and the kitchen was opened up to the garden by means of a glazed wall and a new window. The coach house is the transition between the street and the light-filled glasshouse. One is made aware of connections in this house, whether the thin bridge drawn through the center of the cone, the sculptural plumbing in the bathroom, or the curving waste-pipes of the kitchen sink; or again, the kitchen stairs leading upwards against the glowing colors of what looks like an old frescoed wall (actually made by sealing fragments of old paint). There has been some restrained use of sumptuous materials. The garden terrace is made of blue Belgian limestone set against concrete tiles. There is a sybarite's bathroom: mirrored on two sides, it is otherwise composed of Carrara marble with a basin of blue Brazilian granite. The house incorporates the works of numerous artists, many of whom, like Lili Dujouri and Juan Muñoz, worked with the architects.

Photographs: Kristien Daem & Paul Robbrecht

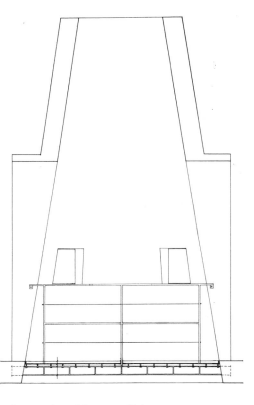

Cross section of the cone of light

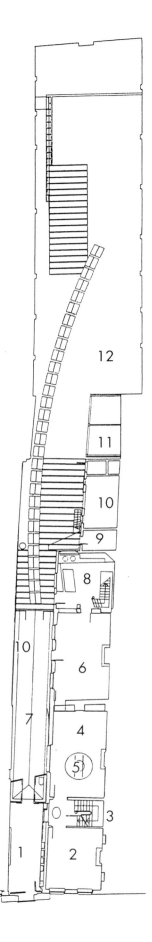

1. Entrance
2. Reception room
3. Stairs to the first floor
4. Library
5. Tower
6. Living-room
7. Conservatory
8. Kitchen
9. Boiler room
10. Closet
11. Garden shed
12. Garden
13. Master bedroom
14. Dressing room
15. Master bathroom
16. Access area between rooms
17. Wardrobe-laundry
18. Games room

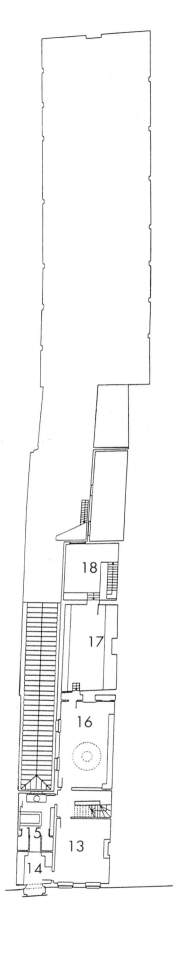

Ground floor plan   First floor plan

Arnaud Goujon Architecte DPLG
Transformed penthouse

Paris, France

In the heart of Paris, the architect Arnaud Goujon transformed an old greenhouse located at the top of a block of flats into a small and comfortable refuge with a terrace and unique views. Conceived as an extension of the loft apartment, this volume would soon become the favorite room of this home. It is a scheme in which the initial volumetrics was respected and a new wooden frame was superimposed on the steel structure. On the exterior, the shingle boards are made of red Canadian cedar, while the interior walls are lined with moabi panels.

The main task for the architect in this rehabilitation –apart from the technical problems– consisted of designing and organizing the different spaces of the apartment, and resolving the problems of execution and assembly of the different materials. The absence of exposed fittings on the wall panels of the interior helps to enlarge and unify the volume of the main room, which opens on both sides onto a terrace of 50 m² covered with a jatoba wood deck and offering spectacular views of the urban landscape.

The interior of this unusual dwelling is composed only of a living room with an open integrated kitchen, in which a chimney is framed between two shelves, and a small bedroom with its bathroom. This room enjoys the benefit of two sources of natural light that illuminate this more private area: a small window in the back wall and a skylight located over the bed. The floor of the interior is made of chestnut parquet covered with white polyurethane paint that reduces the color saturation and brings freshness to the dwelling.

The wood, chosen for its plastic and structural qualities, is used as a double skin: soft and beautiful in the interior and rough and sturdy on the exterior. Thus, although this organic material is set against the urban nature of an environment in which steel is the main component, its form fits well into the geometric pattern of the building.

Photographs: Joel Cariou

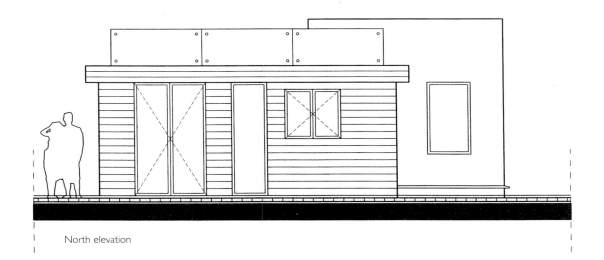

North elevation

The terrace running round this apartment is one of its fundamental elements. The panoramic views of Paris are an additional feature that enhances the architectural work.

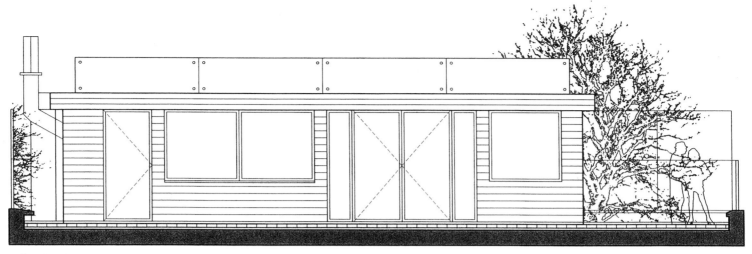

East elevation

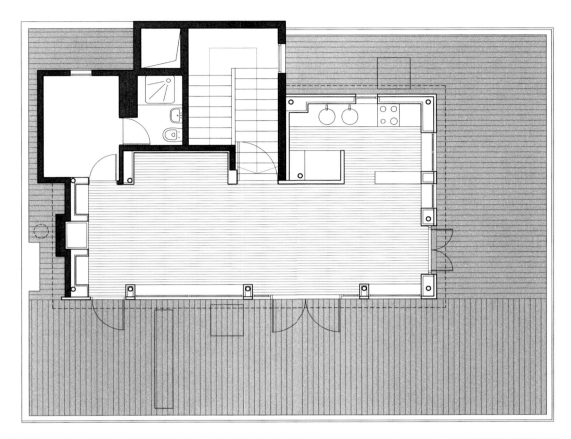

Floor plan

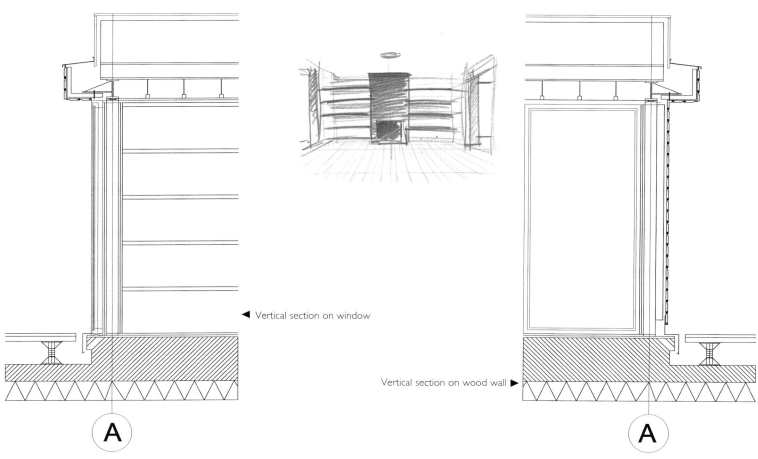

◄ Vertical section on window

Vertical section on wood wall ▶

A

A

Albori Associati
(E. Almagioni, G. Derella, F. Riva)
Casa en Appenninos

Montese, Italy

This old farmhouse of an uncertain age, which has been remodelled several times, is set on a hillside of the Apennines in the region of Módena.

The idea of its new owners was to reduce the bathrooms and bedrooms as far as possible in order to leave the rest of the spaces open and at the disposal of the house. Because it was a building without partitions, in which the interior space coincided with the structure, most of the rooms were on different levels. This pure relationship between space and structures was so beautiful that it was not altered.

Therefore, none of the rooms were divided and the new volumes are characterized by the type of material of the furniture inside them: wood, bricks and stone help to define the uses of the different rooms. The main barn had a certain majesty, with an irregular geometry, a floor area measuring 48 m^2 and a roof that is 6 meters high at its highest point and 2.4 meters at its lowest point. After the demolition of the floor located between the ground floor and the first floor, a large room of double height perfectly illuminated by a long thin skylight was created.

The darkest area in the dwelling was illuminated thanks to the courtyard located at the end of the old barn. In order to adapt this impressive building, originally designed for agricultural use, it was necessary to redesign its lighting and ventilation, without forgetting the enormous possibilities of making openings due to the excellent location. The beautiful views of the valley and the hills surrounding this house were accentuated by the creation of a large terrace in the east wing of the dwelling and by the creation of new windows. These openings led the architects to create a circular layout full of transparencies and unexpected views through the rooms and toward the exterior.

Photographs: Matteo Piazza / Albori

East elevation

Exterior sketch

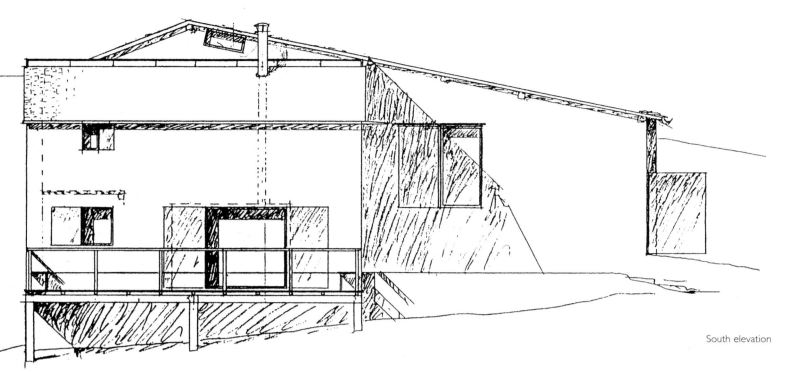

South elevation

The excellent geographical location of this dwelling offers incredible views that are accented by the terrace that was built in the east wing and by the large courtyards.

On the exterior of the dwelling, with one of its main walls sculpted from bare stone, wood and iron were chosen to follow the style of the agricultural buildings in the area.

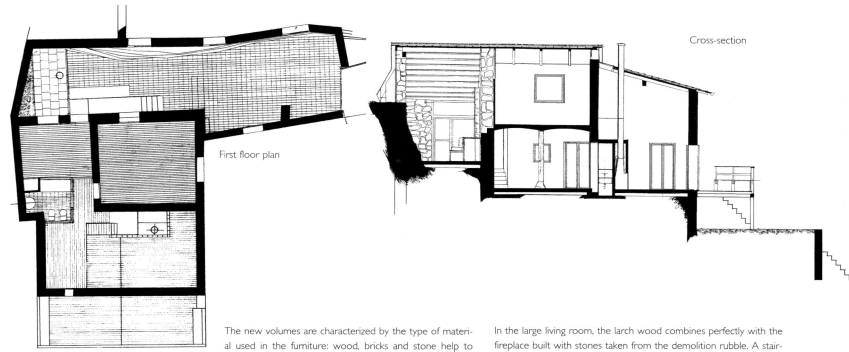

First floor plan

Cross-section

The new volumes are characterized by the type of material used in the furniture: wood, bricks and stone help to define the uses of the different rooms.

In the large living room, the larch wood combines perfectly with the fireplace built with stones taken from the demolition rubble. A staircase rises above the fireplace, with a small toilet underneath it.

The column of the kitchen and the external pergola were made using the beams of the old barn roof.

Carlo Colombo
Loft in Milan

Milan, Italy

In this new layout of this loft from the early 1900s, which had already been adapted for living, Carlo Colombo has kept its nature intact. Moreover, he has combined the informal loft style with a spatial articulation that allows for intimacy.

Primary colors and natural materials have become the expressive elements of this compositional research. The new layout positions fitness areas and spaces for listening to music in the basement. On the ground floor there is a central space to be used as a social area that is set adjacent to the dining-room and kitchen.

A loft platform overlooking the living area contains the bedrooms, the studio and a bath. All this has not produced visual fragmentation: from any point in the house it is possible to glimpse portions of the various spaces.

A horizontal blue band borders the kitchen; a vertical red band marks the volume of the bath. Within the uniformity of the larch wood flooring and the light walls, the first unexpected element is the visual interruption of the blue mosaic tiles. This facing attenuates the high-tech image of the kitchen, which is a seven-meter-long white box. The theatrical effect continues with a tall parallelepiped painted in Pompeii red, with a glass ceiling that contains a raised circular bathtub.

Another volume containing an open shower on the upper level completes the spectacle. The shower overlooks the living area, and seen from below seems almost suspended in space.

Photographs: Santi Caleca

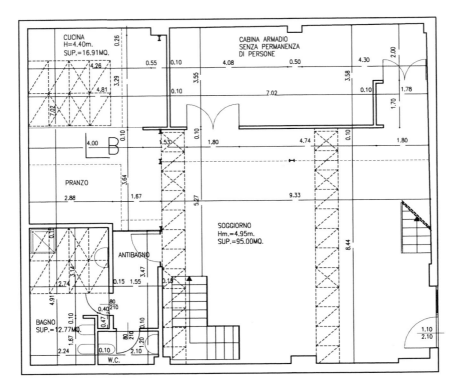

Ground floor plan

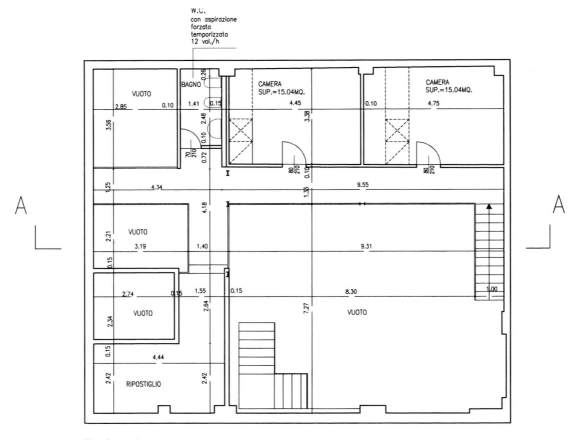

First floor plan

Section A-A

Erected on a turn of the century industrial site, this dwelling conserves the original structure, as seen in the large openings in the roof which uniformly distribute light throughout the home.

Colombo has used basic materials in prime colors for the rehabilitation of the bay. As the distribution resists a rigid fragmentation of spaces, the house is marked by a fluid visual continuity between the various rooms and floors.

Marc van Schuylenbergh
Conversion of Van Schuylenbergh House

Aalst, Belgium

Located in a busy street in the Belgian town of Aalst, the architect Van Schuylenbergh transformed a century-old worker's dwelling into his own home.

In addition to cleaning the facades and opening new windows in the old building, the architect raised a new, long narrow volume that is attached to the old one through an intermediate space in the form of a wedge that follows the curve of the site. This intermediate space is an area of transit in the interior that is well lit from above. The division between the old wing and the new wing is shown by means of a low curving wall.

In the old volume the pure language of the modern intervention is combined with respect for the singularity of some existing elements, such as floor tiles, window frames, fragments of rustic wall face and the old staircase.

The distribution of the rooms has hardly been changed: there are two bedrooms, one situated behind the other, a narrow hall and a staircase.

Another of the most important elements of the new scheme is a raised walkway that communicates the main bedroom with its bathroom, both of which are located on the first floor over each of the two volumes of the dwelling.

Photographs: Jan Caudron Anaklasis

The floors, the doorframes and the old staircase
to the upper floor have been conserved.

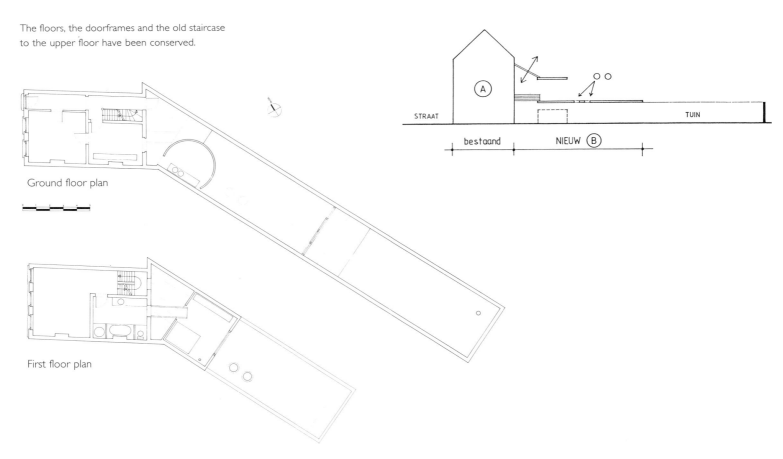

Ground floor plan

First floor plan

STRAAT

A

TUIN

bestaand   NIEUW B

Derek Wylie Architecture
Lee House

Clerkenwell, London, UK

In this block in Clerkenwell, a fashionable district of London, the architect had acquired a complex composed of a Victorian building with a shop on the ground floor and a workshop at the end of the court in order to work and live there with his family.

Surrounded by buildings, the narrow and deep plot had very little light and even fewer outside views. The project consisted, therefore, in creating fluid spaces in the existing structure and optimizing the entrance of natural light by creating an interior court framed by the L-shaped ground plan. To take full advantage of this quiet space, floor-to-ceiling sliding glass panels are used and the court becomes the natural exterior elongation of the living room, whose furniture is equipped with rollers for a highly flexible layout.

Light penetrates the heart of the dwelling through skylights, which are covered by a wood-clad steel structure, that have been installed above the kitchen and the mezzanine. Furthermore, the set-back alignment of the facade defined a space of transition between the street and the office and authorized the use of glass paving that provides direct lighting for the bathroom situated in the basement.

In many ways, glass facilitates the circuit of light from skylights toward the inside of the house. In the mezzanine covered with a glass roof, the floor is made of strips of glass and oak that constitute a semi-translucent floor. Outside, the small balcony also has a glass floor in order to avoid casting too much shade on the facade and the court.

This attention to the trajectory of light is found even in the kitchen elements clad in aluminum, of which the high cupboard doors are profiled in order to allow the light to slip from the glass roof toward the working area.

The materials used respond to criteria of simplicity and hardiness. An oak parquet laid on the whole ground floor including the staircase of the entrance accentuates the spatial continuity of this level, with the exception of a part of the kitchen in which the limestone paving of the court continues along the working plane. The two new staircases with oak-clad steps are supported by steel structures. This structure is of welded plates in the mezzanine staircase, and features a tapered mast for the staircase at the rear.

The project is sober and functional; the existing brick walls have been conserved as they were or simply painted blank, a testimony to the history of places that is pursued by the architect.

Photographs: Nick Kane

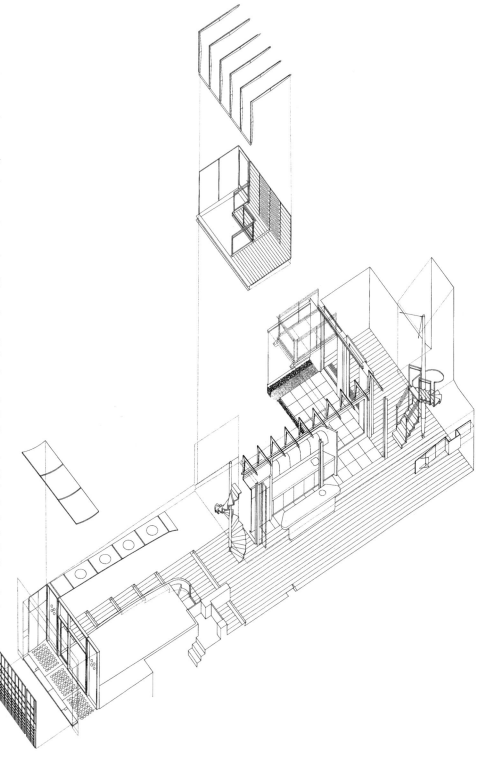

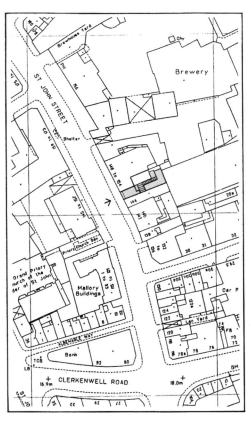

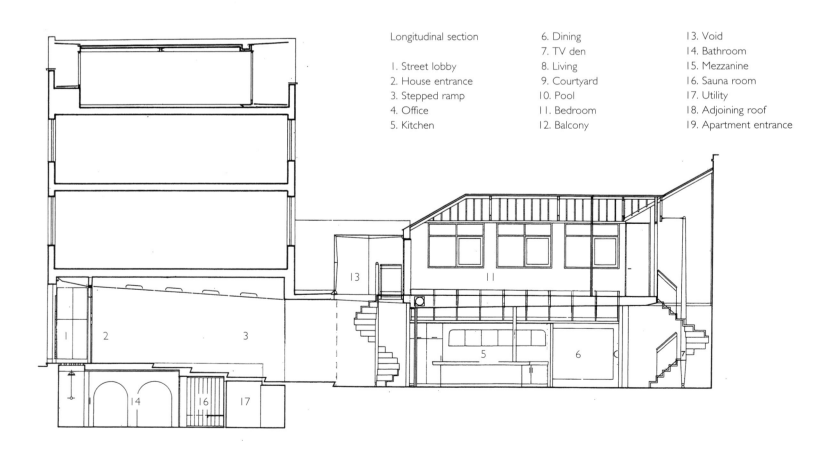

Longitudinal section

1. Street lobby
2. House entrance
3. Stepped ramp
4. Office
5. Kitchen
6. Dining
7. TV den
8. Living
9. Courtyard
10. Pool
11. Bedroom
12. Balcony
13. Void
14. Bathroom
15. Mezzanine
16. Sauna room
17. Utility
18. Adjoining roof
19. Apartment entrance

In order to maximize the entry of natural light in all the rooms of the studio and the house, an inner L-shaped courtyard was created and becomes the focus of the structure. To take full advantage of this quiet space, floor-to-ceiling sliding glass panels are used and the court becomes the natural exterior prolongation of the living room, where the furniture is equipped with rollers for a highly flexible layout..

First floor plan

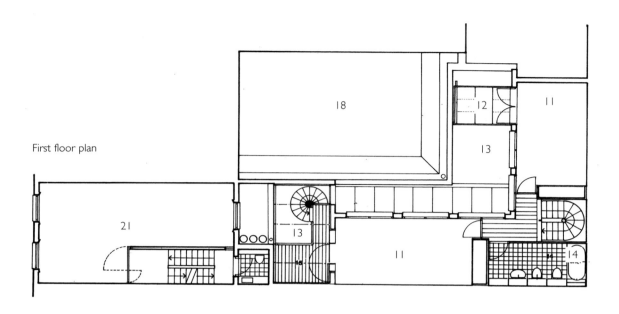

Ground floor plan

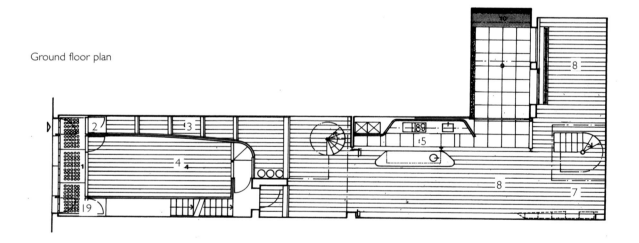

Basement floor plan

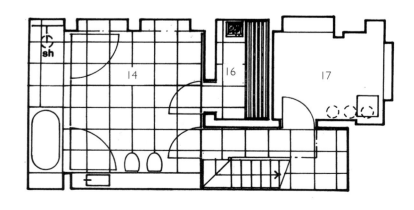

The staircases: the alternate use of oak and translucent glass panels in the floor of the mezzanine enhances the sensation of light on the lower floors.

Terver, Couvert & Beddock
Villa Schumann-Sizaret

Chevanny, France

In this restructuring and conversion of an agricultural building into a dwelling, an analysis of the framework and financial reasons led the architects to develop a sequential project in three phases that would successively occupy the three arches of the building.

The house (in bare stonework) is composed of three parts, each housing different functions. The first arch contains the Winter House, which is isolated, heated and covers all the basic necessities. The second one is for intermediate activities, such as indoor and outdoor functions in the spring and autumn, and features a veranda and an internal garden. The third arch was designed to encompass, later, the Summer House, which would also contain supplementary bedrooms.

The existing materials such as the stone of the window breast and the wood lintels were respected. The internal intervention in the first phase consists of the creation of two technical wood boxes, one per level, housing all the building's functional requirements (cooking, toilet, storage, heating, etc.). These boxes occupy a central position, which permits the use of their four sides and allows a corresponding future subdivision of the initial internal volume free from the basic functional constraints. The entry, in the central arch, is marked by a protruding wood module that allows an integration and an interaction with the garden and the surrounding orchard. The natural lighting of this bay is achieved thanks to the use of glass tiles on the roofing in the form of an opus incertum. The third arch will be carried out at a later stage.

Photographs: T. Delhaste

Site plan

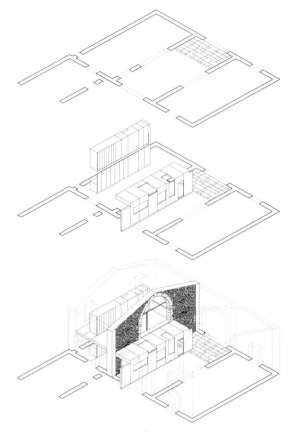

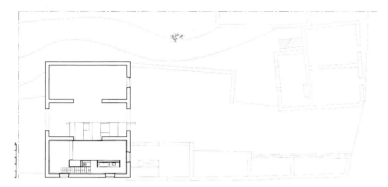

Upper floor plan

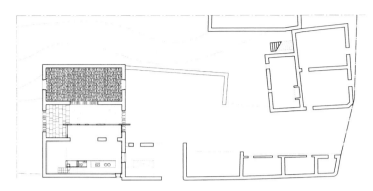

Lower floor plan

The first phase of the project consisted of the creation of two blocks of wood and glass that house the basic functions of a dwelling. These blocks have been located in a central position to allow the exploration of their four sides and the free distribution of the interior space.

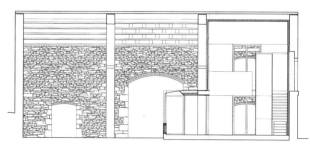

Cross-section

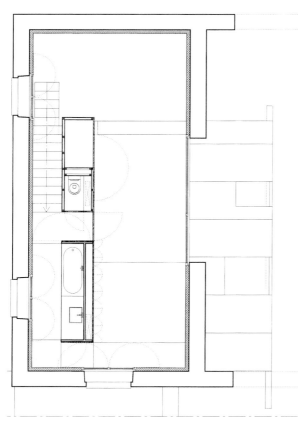

Upper floor plan

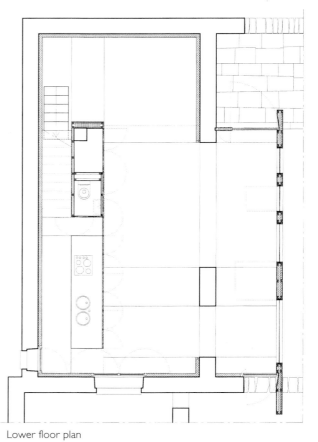

Lower floor plan

234

Giovanni Scheibler
Loft Conversion in Zurich

Zurich, Switzerland

In converting the loft space in this house, the aim was to create extra living space and to bring more light into the top floor flat, while respecting the characteristic early 20th-century outward appearance of the building. Ecological and economic factors were also taken into consideration. The architects created a central hall, lit from above by a new roof light set in the ridge of the mansard roof, 7m above the hall floor. There are no fittings that block the path of light: even the gallery floor is of clear glass. Light can also filter through translucent walls into the rooms bordering the hall. Sliding partition elements further help to create space and versatility, in contrast to the usual narrow confines of such flats. The materials used for the new hall are clearly legible against the existing building structure. Anthracite-colored metal, chromed steel and glass stand next to plaster walls and wood. The fine lines of the elements of the hall complement the theme of transparency. The girders supporting the gallery are pairs of tensioned RHS-sections, resting on brackets on the mansard structure.
The cable bracing eliminates any vibrations along the slim sections. The safety glass flooring sheets rest on a double layer of rubber to reduce noise. Chromed steel is used for the handrail and the horizontal cabling. The frame of the sliding partitions is of narrow square tube sections. Between the glazing layers is white glass lining welded to the panes at the side.

Photographs: Alex Spichale

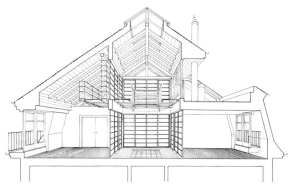

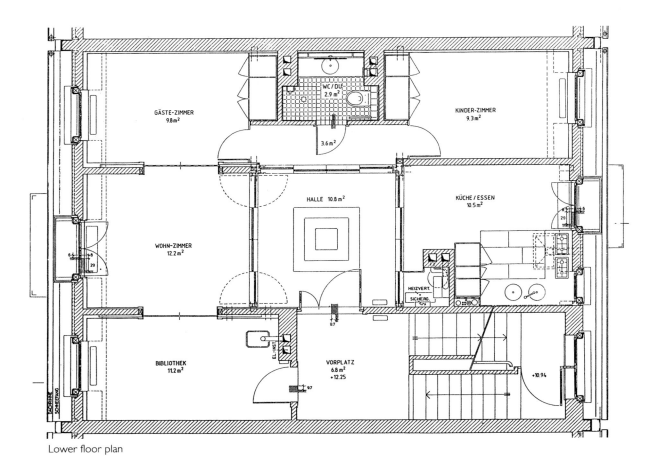

GÄSTE-ZIMMER
9.8 m²

WC/DU
2.9 m²

KINDER-ZIMMER
9.3 m²

3.6 m²

WOHN-ZIMMER
12.2 m²

HALLE 10.8 m²

KÜCHE / ESSEN
10.5 m²

HEIZVERT.

SICHERG.

BIBLIOTHEK
11.2 m²

VORPLATZ
6.8 m²
+12.25

EL-INST

+10.94

Lower floor plan

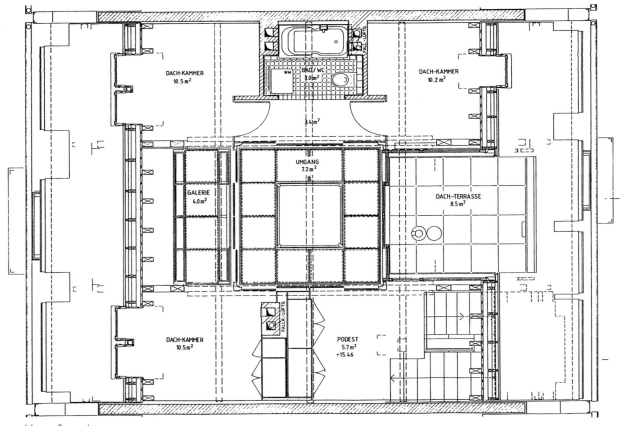

DACH-KAMMER
10.5 m²

BAD/WC
3.0 m²

DACH-KAMMER
10.2 m²

3.4 m²

UMGANG
7.2 m²

GALERIE
4.0 m²

DACH-TERRASSE
8.5 m²

DACH-KAMMER
10.5 m²

PODEST
5.7 m²
+15.46

Upper floor plan

238

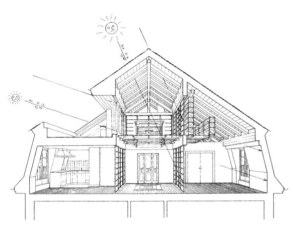

The dwelling is organized around a central hall that is top-lit by a skylight.

The light comes through the translucent glass panels into the rooms surrounding the central hall.

The materials used to build the central hall (steel and glass) are easily recognizable, contrasting with the existing structure of the building.

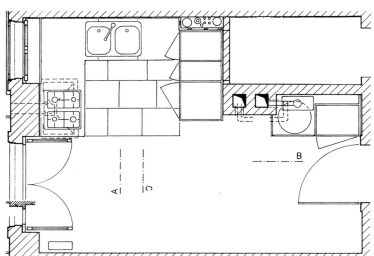

Kitchen floor plan

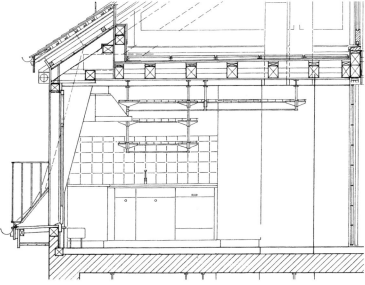

Section through the kitchen

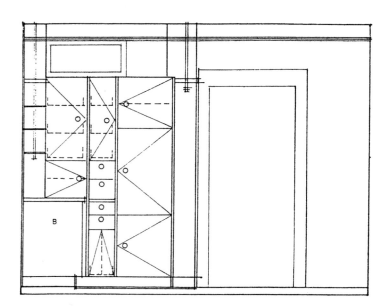

Interior elevations

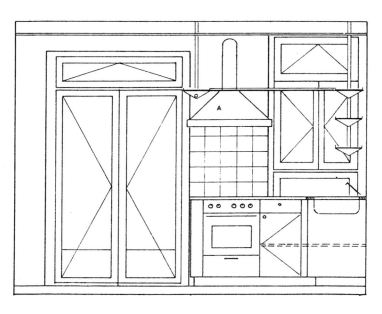

The kitchen, reached directly through the central hall, has been completely redesigned to create two sharply differentiated environments within it: the work space and a small eating area. A system of stainless steel suspended shelves provide visual organization of the space.

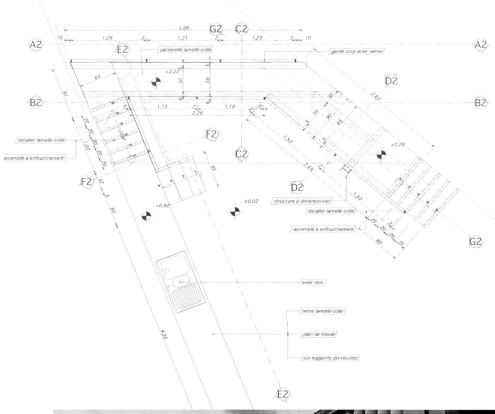

Jean-Pierre Lévêque
Maison Rue Compans

Paris, France

This building, an old laboratory built in the thirties, was transformed into an inhabitable space after twenty years. It is located in a complex fabric of plots, a kind of residual space in the form of an isosceles triangle between two five-story blocks.

For the rehabilitation of this small dwelling of 80 m², the brief was to optimize its habitability and to rediscover in the space a clear legibility and its initial constitution as a building suspended over a covered exterior.

The layout offered the possibility of creating a multi-purpose space defined by the exterior and interior elements. The ground floor was left completely open in order to allow the exterior, consisting of the covered courtyard, to be extended completely into the house. Inside this covered exterior, a differentiated structure containing the kitchen was inserted. This "box" is completely open within the continuous layout of the floor, walls and ceiling, thus giving the dwelling a distinguished appearance.

The exterior of this volume is secured by means of the lower part of the room, and by the pillar that supports it. The house is therefore suspended, with the areas that require greater domestic privacy, such as the bedrooms and the bathroom, at the top. All the spaces were connected to each other by means of a wooden strip. This begins as the main envelope of the kitchen, becomes the staircase that gives access to the first floor and ends in a wide bookcase before leading to the bedrooms. This "Ariadne's thread", ensures maximum fluidity, multiplying all possible points of view in the area of the dining room and the kitchen in the ascent to the first level, in which all the dimensions of the space that one moves through are apparent.

The basement is accessed by a long flight of stairs that is partially covered by a glass panel. This opening provides natural lighting for the office located in the basement, and accentuates the effect of inclusion of the kitchen volume in the ground floor. the requalification of the environmental context.

Photographs: Hervé Abbadie

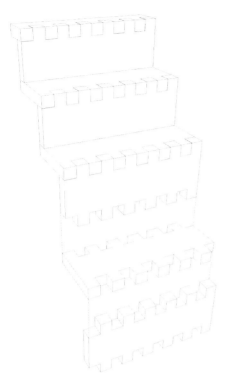

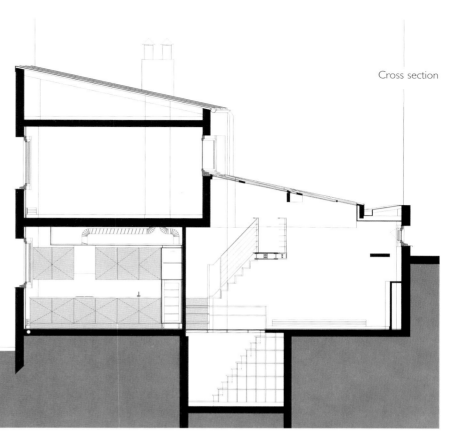

Cross section, kitchen

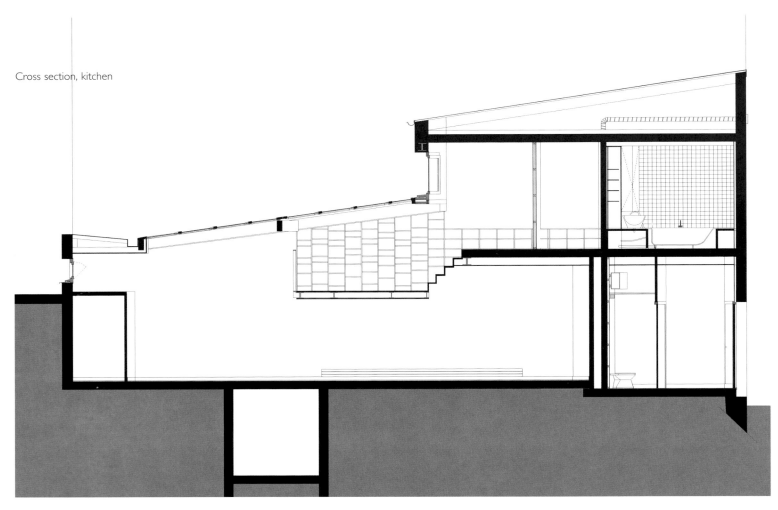

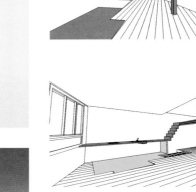

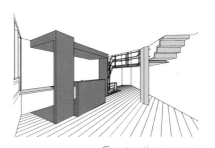

Construction process

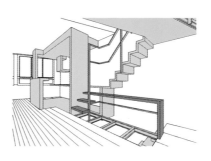

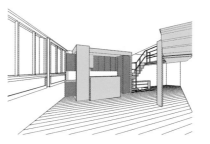

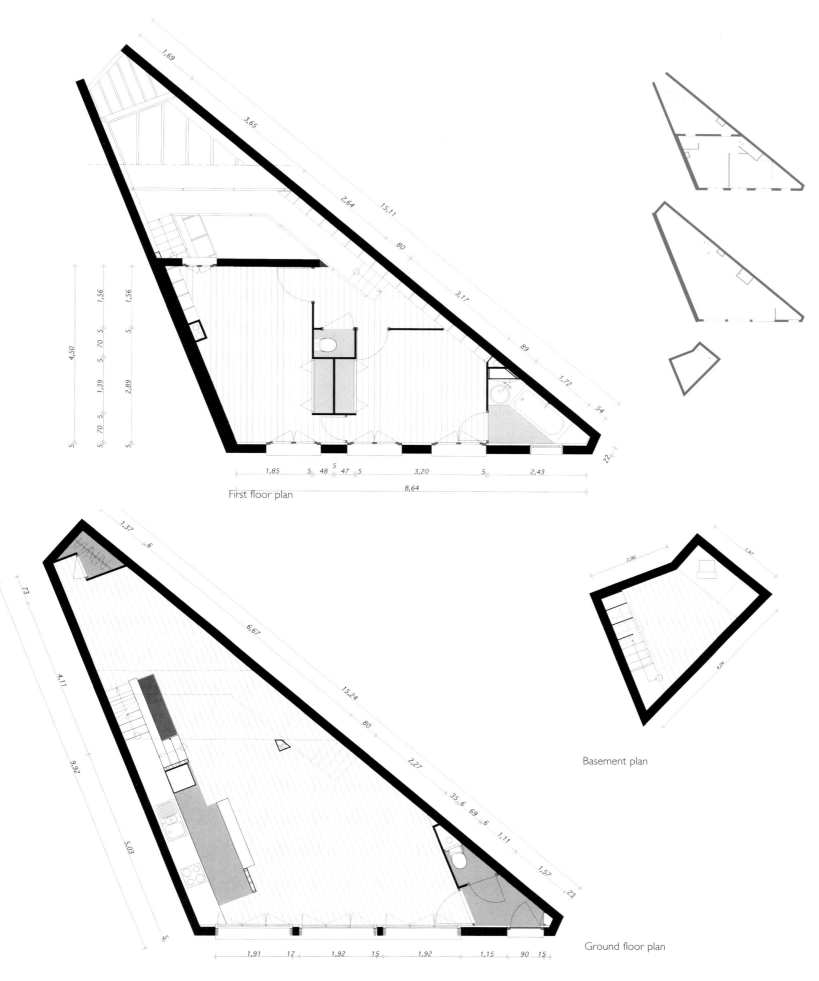

First floor plan

Basement plan

Ground floor plan

249

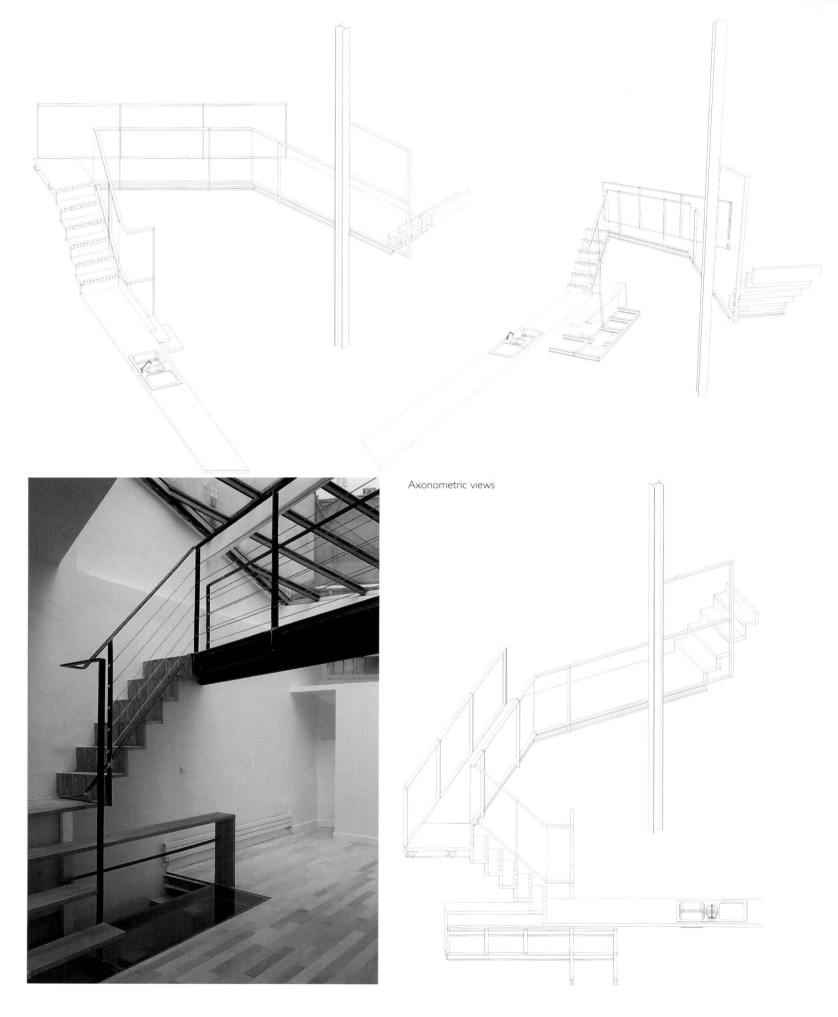

Axonometric views

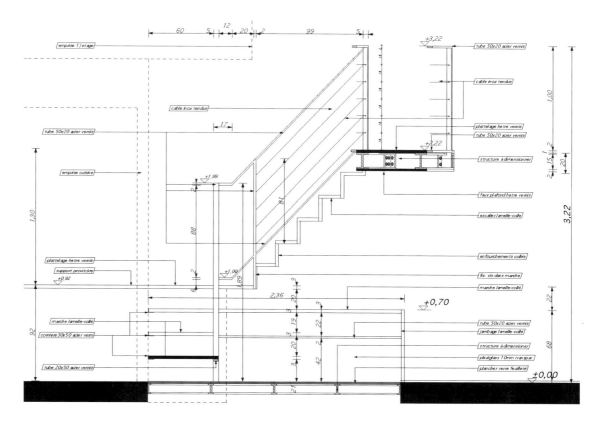

The walkway —which serves as an access to the main room— maintains a continuity with the staircase and the kitchen module.

Mauro Galantino & Federico Poli (Studio 3)
Casa sul lago d'Orta

Orta S. Giulio, Italy

This unusual building is located in the Gothic district of an Italian town not far from Milan. The vertical nature of the house is conserved almost intact thanks to the two medieval walls that define the boundaries and the jetty.

Before the restoration, the building was in ruins, the ceilings were deteriorated and a large part of the foundations rested on the sandy bed of the lake. According to studies, this building was partly rebuilt in the 14th century, though the jetty was built in the 19th century. At first sight, it seems to be a simple rehabilitation: a productive residential microcosm. The domestic areas, such as the bedrooms and the living room, are organized vertically in the north "tower", while below the former cowshed, the henhouse, the garden and the jetty are organized in relation to the lake.

The restoration of this house —used as a second residence— respected the stipulations for the conservation of the cultural heritage with regard to volumes, walls and material. The work was based on two objectives: to adapt the residential structure to new functions, and to obey the building regulations on the use of materials without sacrificing the possibility of a creating a new perception of the rehabilitated parts.

The result was a residential space composed of a living room of double height forming a horizontal, parallelepiped space with a covered jetty at the south end and a "tower" containing the living areas at the other end.

Photographs: Alberto Muciaccia

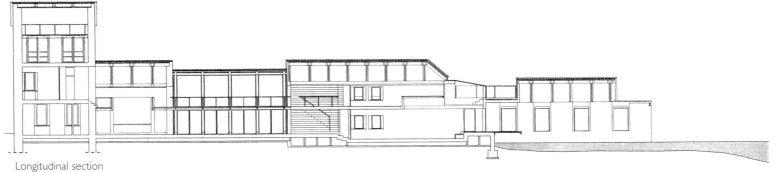

Longitudinal section

Ground floor plan

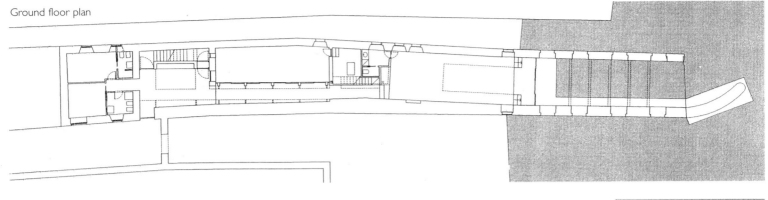

First floor plan

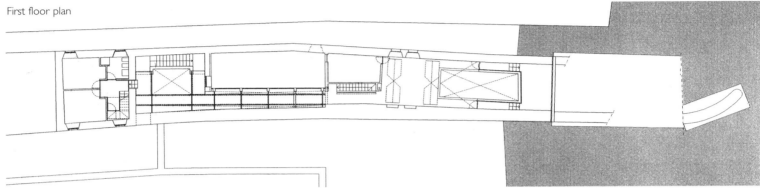

Section through living-room

1. Roof
2. Unpolished gneiss cornice
3. Plaster-type facing with vermiculite
4. Cladding of horizontal polished gneiss panels
5. Varnished steel railing, 4x4 "T" horizontal, 4x4 "H" vertical
6. 5x5x5 grill
7. Staircase with polished solid gneiss steps on hollow-brick partitions
8. Cladding of horizontal polished gneiss panels
9. Protection grill
10. Breather of the ventilated floor
11. Unpolished gneiss tile
12. Grave
13. Wall with 6/6/4 double glazing and varnished galvanized steel frame

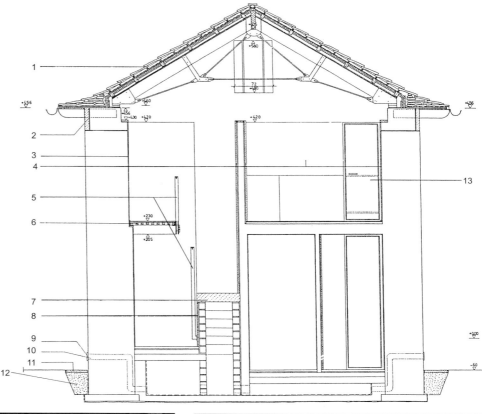

The jetty acts as an entrance door to this "residential microcosm". It was built in the 19th century to extend the horizontal volume 61of this medieval building.

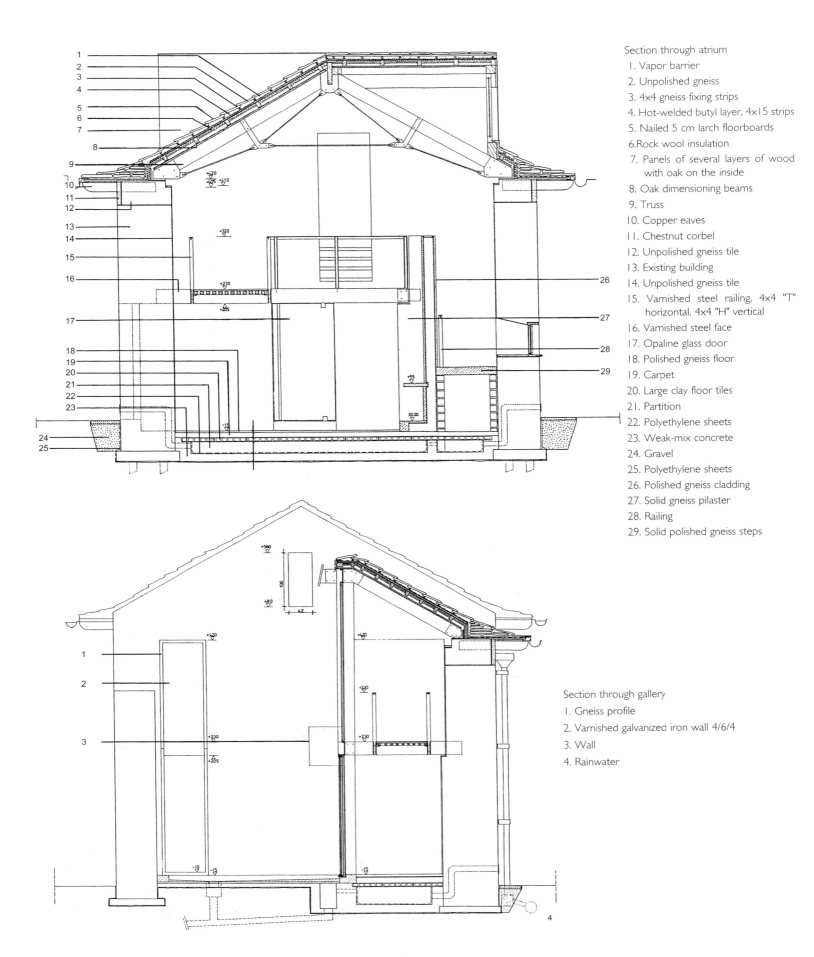

Section through atrium
1. Vapor barrier
2. Unpolished gneiss
3. 4x4 gneiss fixing strips
4. Hot-welded butyl layer, 4x15 strips
5. Nailed 5 cm larch floorboards
6. Rock wool insulation
7. Panels of several layers of wood with oak on the inside
8. Oak dimensioning beams
9. Truss
10. Copper eaves
11. Chestnut corbel
12. Unpolished gneiss tile
13. Existing building
14. Unpolished gneiss tile
15. Varnished steel railing, 4x4 "T" horizontal, 4x4 "H" vertical
16. Varnished steel face
17. Opaline glass door
18. Polished gneiss floor
19. Carpet
20. Large clay floor tiles
21. Partition
22. Polyethylene sheets
23. Weak-mix concrete
24. Gravel
25. Polyethylene sheets
26. Polished gneiss cladding
27. Solid gneiss pilaster
28. Railing
29. Solid polished gneiss steps

Section through gallery
1. Gneiss profile
2. Varnished galvanized iron wall 4/6/4
3. Wall
4. Rainwater

Section through building

1. Roof
2. 2.5 cm oak-veneered plywood boards
3. Railing
4. Unpolished gneiss tile
5. Teak boards
6. Floorboards
7. Drop ceiling of 2-5 cm oak-finish plywood boards
8. Iron wall, "H" 4×4 horizontal, "T" 4×4 vertical
9. Teak boards
10. Oak floorboards
11. Oak beam
12. Fancoil

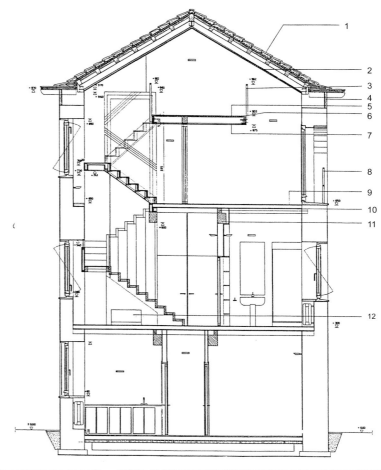

The staircase communicates the floors of the "tower" located at the north end of the residence which houses the bedroom. At the south end is the jetty facing Lake Orta.

Littow architectes
Paris 6e

Paris, France

This apartment occupies the last two floors of a Parisian property built in the 17th century. These last two floors were probably built more recently to house two simpler apartments for the servants. It was later decided to join them to form a single apartment. After a meticulous study of the technical limits of this conversion, the challenge consisted in obtaining a space that was as open as possible. All the existing elements that limited the views or the natural lighting were reduced without sacrificing the hierarchy of the spaces and the structure of the inhabitable areas. It was thus attempted to create subtle and delicate borders that could be adjusted. They are like visual borders that allow for different interpretations. The dining room is isolated from the other rooms by glazed walls, allowing in the natural light from the inner courtyard and from the openings in the guest room. The kitchen forms an integral part of the living room, although it is completely concealed by a set of folding wooden panels, so the appearance of the apartment varies according to the time of day and the needs of its occupants.

The abundance of exposed pillars and wooden props, many of which were completely rotten, called for special treatment and some were eliminated or replaced. The brick walls of the street facade were stripped and according to age-old techniques, showing a craftsman's touch that gives new value to the building.

In the upper room the drop ceilings were removed to reveal magnificent woodwork. The same procedure was applied to the guest room, where a small mezzanine was installed to the right of the volume of the old covered structure. Inside the dwelling, the new spaces that have been created reveal more about the demolition and the subtle unification than about the construction itself. Composing with the existing elements was a priority, but the question was to define what could be changed, what had to be conserved and how to deal with it. The first rule was that the original structures should be the dominant ones, the new elements only playing a secondary role.

The furniture was designed by the architect and made specially for these spaces with the aim of creating a relaxing atmosphere.

Photographs: Pekka Littow

Cross-section

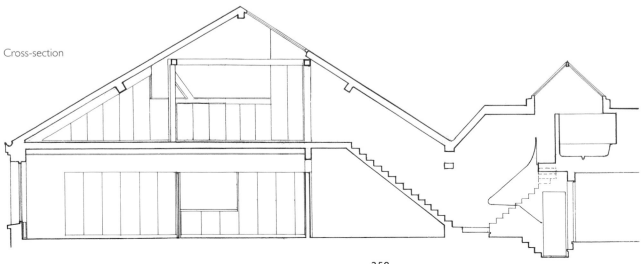

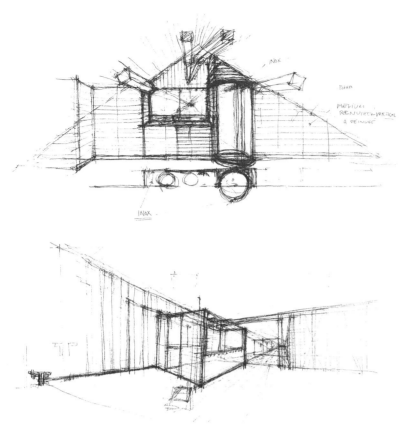

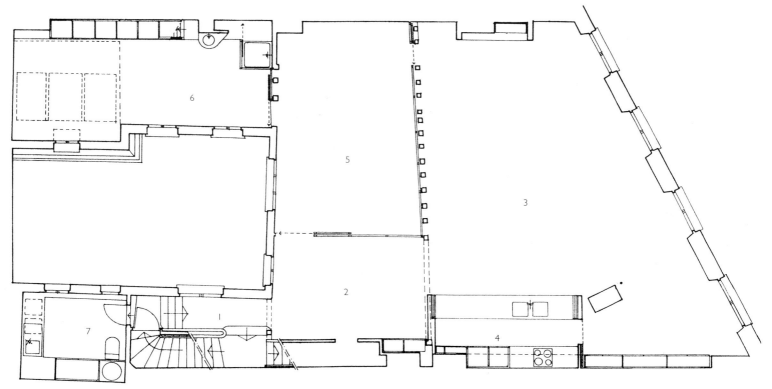

First floor plan
1. Entrance
2. Hall
3. Living room
4. Kitchen
5. Dining room
6. Guestroom
7. Laundry

Upper floor plan
8. Master bedroom
9. Bathroom
10. Toilet
11. Mezzanine

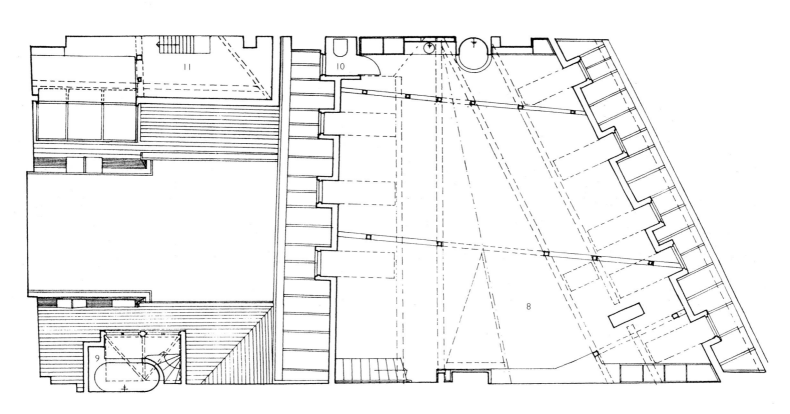

Fraser Brown MacKenna
Derbyshire St. Residence

London, UK

Following personal recommendations, Fraser Brown MacKenna Architects were chosen by the client to design a new house in an abandoned shopping area of Hackney.

Although finally the site was not purchased, the plans for the scheme were well received and included in the RIBA'S "First Sight" exhibition in 1995. The client then asked Fraser Brown MacKenna to restore the two upper floors of a converted loft in Bethnal Green. A dramatic barrel-vaulted Perspex roof had been added to the building, but spaces within were subdivided and darkened.

A translucent floor was used in a space of double height, the upper floor being used as the main area with the kitchen and dining room. The lower floor was stripped and opened to achieve a large flexible environment for sleeping, working and living. On this floor, a ten meter long, full height Plexiglas screen, divides storage and utility spaces from the main circulation and living areas in the building. It provides a bright, clean plane in contrast with the large expanse of the restored floorboards. The light is reflected in it, causing effects of brightness and shade that give the impression that the light comes alive as one moves.

This screen can be moved to modify the space, thus creating a new area for sleeping, talking or relaxing and allowing the space to adapt to the needs of the owners. The screen employs a bold language expressed in the stainless steel socket cap head screws and aluminumT-sections. Against the screen, the simple geometry of the copper cladding of the storage area reveals within its natural patina a hundred hues to play against the subtle shadows of light. The simple form of screen, box, sink and fin walls formed from glass blocks or perforated metal set within acknowledges the space and what it had once been.

Photographs: Nick Hufton

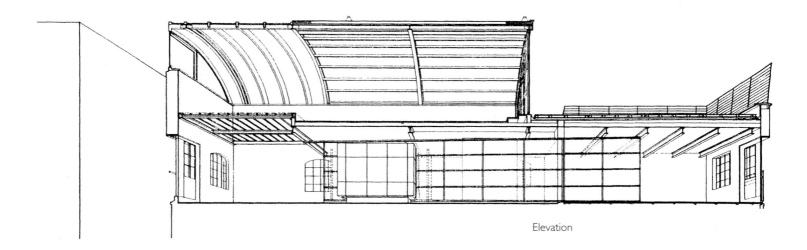

Elevation

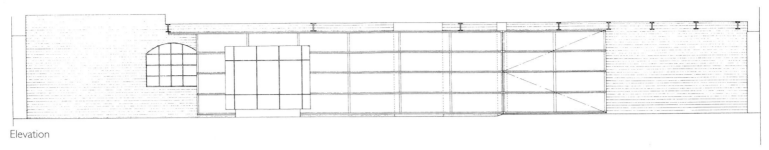

Elevation

The wood floor, the staircase and the original roof beams reveal the age of this apartment, while at the same time giving it a sober and elegant character.

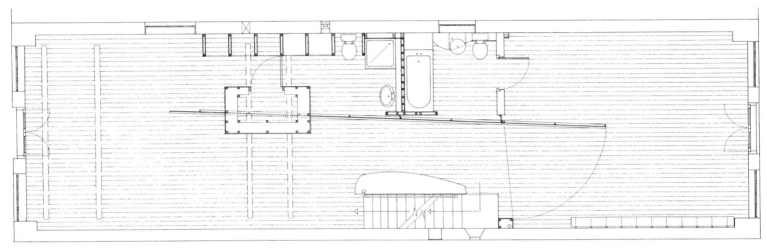

Ground floor plan

A copper box embedded in the Plexiglas screen acts as a cupboard. The reflections and textures of this rough-finished element show the care taken by the architects in the aesthetic use of materials.

First floor plan

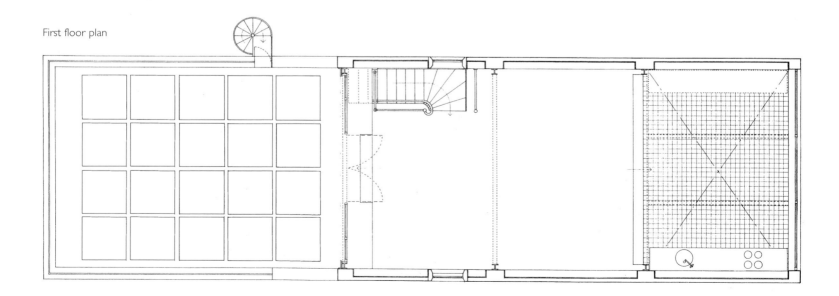

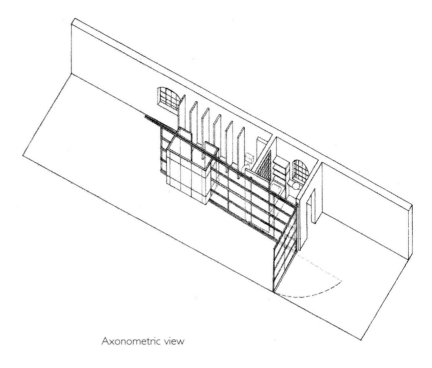

Axonometric view

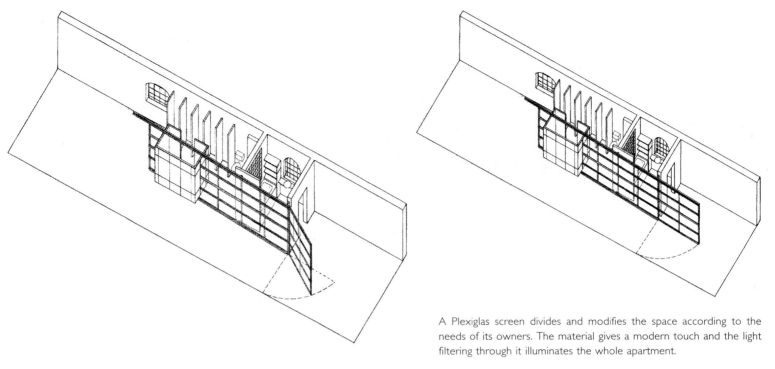

A Plexiglas screen divides and modifies the space according to the needs of its owners. The material gives a modern touch and the light filtering through it illuminates the whole apartment.

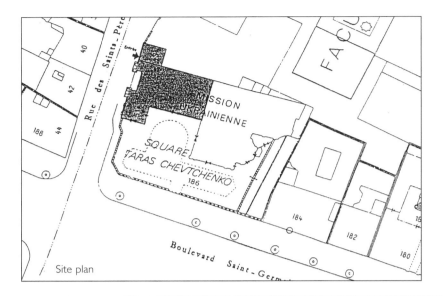

Site plan

Georges Maurios
Rue des Saint-Pères

Paris, France

For the conversion of this building, the architect aimed to create a privileged space: a group of perfectly equipped apartments in which the small dimensions were no impediment to the creation of a space for working and living comfortably, and in which modernity was no obstacle to maintaining all the characteristics of a traditional habitat.

Due to the conditions of the existing space, the main question for the architect consisted of choosing the best construction method. The brief was to design five apartments of 4.16 m height, although due to the exceptional nature of the location, it was immediately suggested to double the number of spaces by creating duplex apartments. However, the different elements had to be prevented from interfering with each other, bearing in mind the limited floor area and the need to increase the impression of space and seek greater potential use. To achieve this, the duplex system offered the possibility of overlapping spaces with minimum interference, though it called for a careful design to fit the volumes into the dimensions of the building and great care in the construction of the interior.

The spatial relation between the staircase and the office made it possible to create this impression of a vital space on the ground floor, which is all open plan and incorporates a spacious office.

Photographs: Olivier Wogenscky

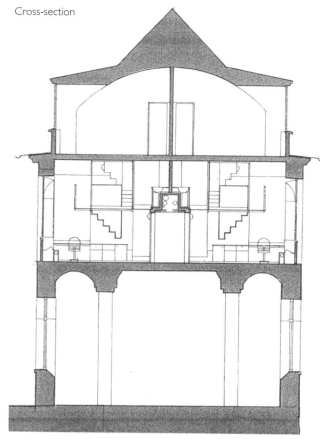

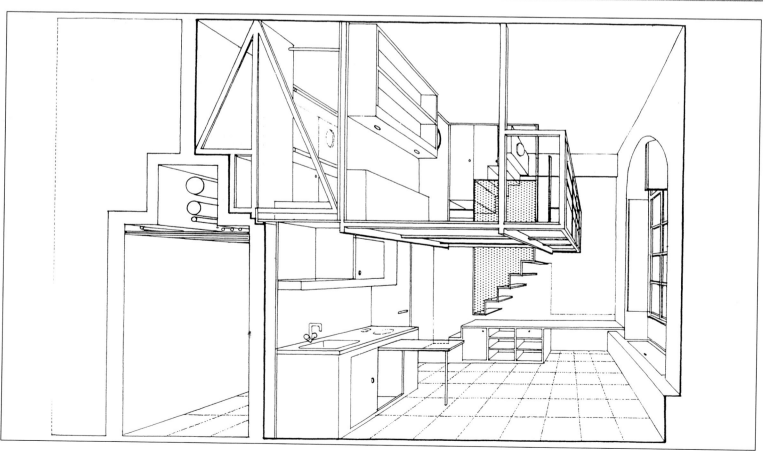

1. Desk
2. Kitchen
3. Bedroom
4. Toilet
5. Bench
6. Fitted cupboard
7. Water heater
8. Conduit
9. Void
10. Technical conduit
11. Common corridor

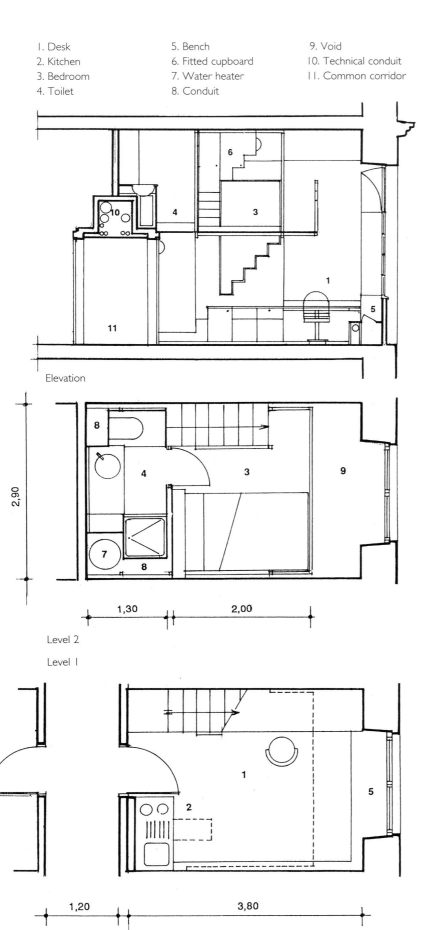

Elevation

2,90

1,30   2,00

Level 2

Level 1

1,20   3,80

273

1. Maisonette
2. Studio
3. Offices
4. Reception
5. Distribution boards
6. Technical conduit

Space was saved by the incorporation of a bench by the window (shown here in the background) that doubles as storage space and a two-sided articulation block in the kitchen that also forms an impromptu dining table.

Eduard Broto
Attic at Eixample

Barcelona, Spain

This project by the architect Eduard Broto consisted of reha-
bilitating an attic located in a 'modernista' (art-nouveau) building in the "right-hand side" of the Barcelona Eixample district.
Before the restoration, the attic consisted of a single room
used for storage, and a large terrace.

The scheme made full use of the possibilities of the premises
whilst making a minimum number of changes. The traditional
character of the building has been conserved in the transformation of an obsolete space into a modern functional building.

A wooden element similar to a cupboard was created. It separates and organizes the different zones into which the
dwelling is divided. The generous height of the ceiling made it
possible to install a half-floor, thus gaining habitable space.

The living room is situated at the front of the dwelling, and may
be fully opened onto the adjoining terrace. The walls and windows of this main room were decorated with the same 'modernista' floral motif that is found on the stairs of the building.

At the rear of the dwelling are the kitchen, bathroom and a small
bedroom. All of the rooms are interconnected, separated only by
a sliding door system. The bathroom, a particularly bright and
spacious room, is separated from the rest by means of a stained
glass partition.

Photographs: Eugeni Pons

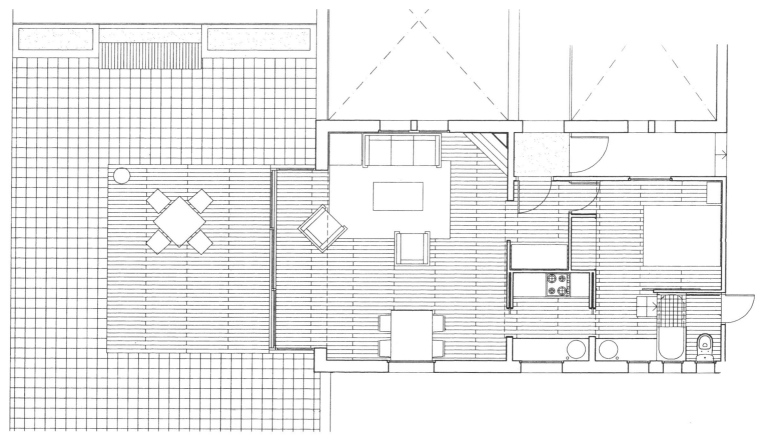

278

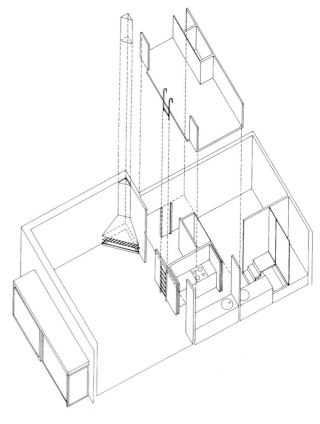

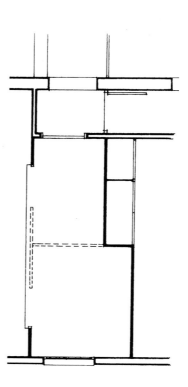

Christa Prantl & Alexander Runser
Lanzendorfer Mühle

Mistelbach, Austria

In this low-budget conversion of a baroque mill located in a small village some 50 km from Vienna, the brief was to establish a large living area on the roof floor of the old storage building, and to create space for a doctor's surgery on the main level. The main level of the residential building was to be remodeled to house the private rooms and a small apartment.

The baroque façade was renovated, and the partly-destroyed walls protecting the gardens east and west of the building were re-erected. The facade of the cellar level on the East Side was excavated and found to be an arcade. It is now the entrance to the doctor's surgery. On the west side of the building, a new entrance to the living area was made, providing access to a staircase, which leads up to the new living area in the roof space.

The main intervention was the installation of a new concrete object at the intersection of the storage building and the long residential building. Four walls, consisting of plates of bare reinforced concrete, define the way into the building. They create a link between the entrance, the private rooms, the new living space on the roof floor, and the surgery in the former storage building. This modern element connects, divides and opens up the older structure, without destroying it.

Two 20 m² glass windows in the roof admit light into the entrance hall, the large living space on the roof floor and the rooms of the surgery. Eight soundproof glass doors separate the surgery from the living space. This, and the soundproof construction of the ceiling, prevent conflict between the inhabitants' living and working spaces. The bare concrete structure helps to separate the living and working areas visually. The physical bulk of this material stores heat, an important factor in maintaining a well-balanced room climate. The space under the glass roof did not require solar protection.

Photographs: Margherita Spiluttini

282

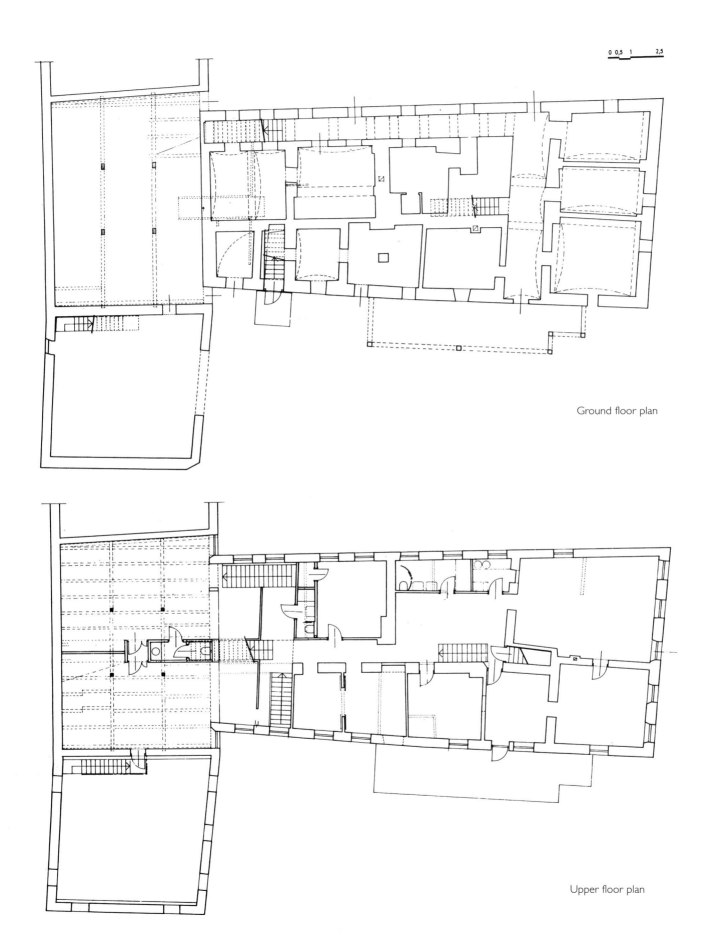

Ground floor plan

Upper floor plan

284

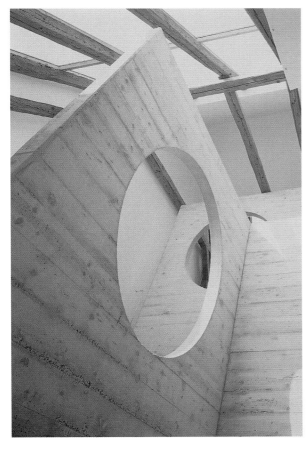

West elevation

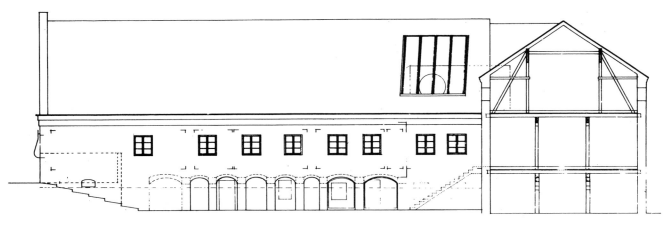

East elevation

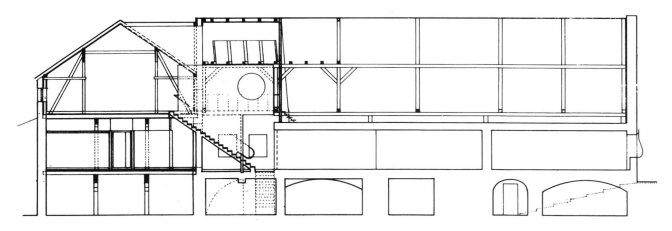

Longitudinal section

The magnificent assembled wooden structure that supports the sloping roof has been fully restored. The contrast between the varnished wood and the white walls highlights its beauty.

Longitudinal section

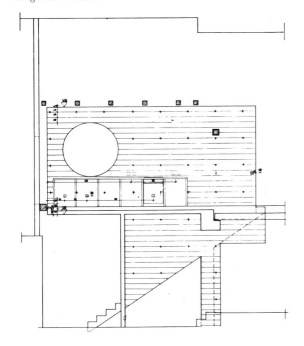

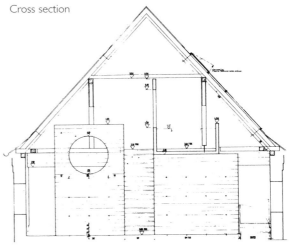

The living area situated under the roof receives plenty of natural light through the two large skylights.

Michael Graves
Graves Residence: The Warehouse

Princeton, USA

The home of one of the most representative figures of post-modernist architecture, Michael Graves, is a converted warehouse, built in 1926 by Italian stonemasons who built several masonry buildings at Princeton University. It was built in a typical Tuscan vernacular style using hollow clay tiles, bricks and stucco. The L-shaped building, originally divided into many storage cells, was renovated in stages.

The north wing is entered through an external courtyard that was once a truck-loading bay, and includes a living room, a dining room and a long, narrow, overwhelmingly tall library with a garden terrace on the ground floor, and a master bedroom and study on the first floor. The architect retained the original concrete flooring, treating it, however, to resemble stone.

The use of daylight throughout the house deliberately reinforces the understanding of particular rooms and suggests continuity between the building and the surrounding natural landscape. Rather than flooding the house with the diffuse light of the outdoors, Graves' more selective approach has the effect of energizing the interiors with a dynamic sense of the time of day and year.

The house is carefully furnished with an extensive collection of books, objects, furniture and art, creating convivial settings that convey a sense of habitation and reinforce the feeling of domesticity. The exterior pink stucco, the interior decoration, the niches and columns all come together to artfully enhance the classical inspiration of the original building.

Photographs: Michael Graves & Marek Bulaj

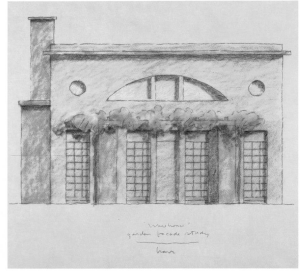

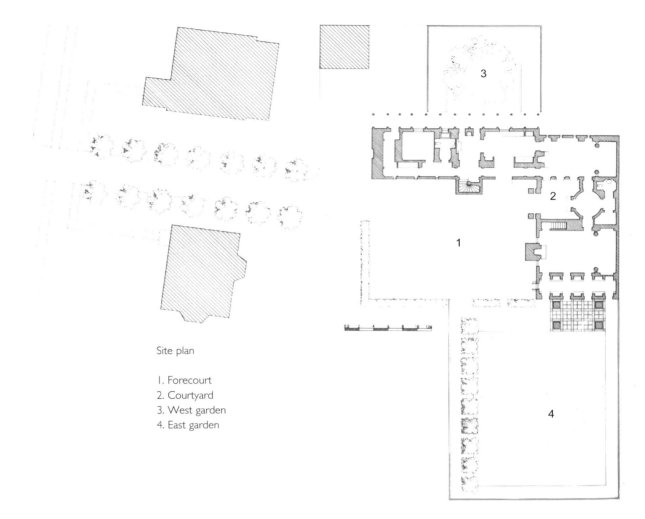

Site plan

1. Forecourt
2. Courtyard
3. West garden
4. East garden

East-west section of north wing

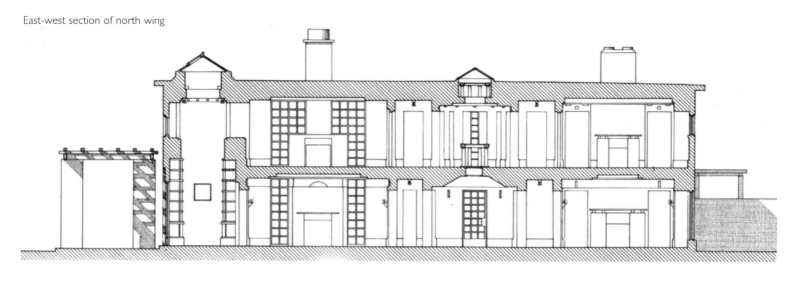

North-south section of west wing and north wing

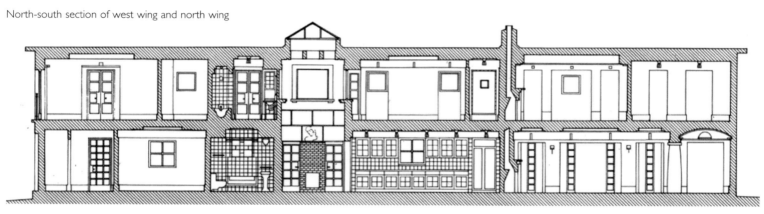

North wing, section of entry, courtyard and foyer

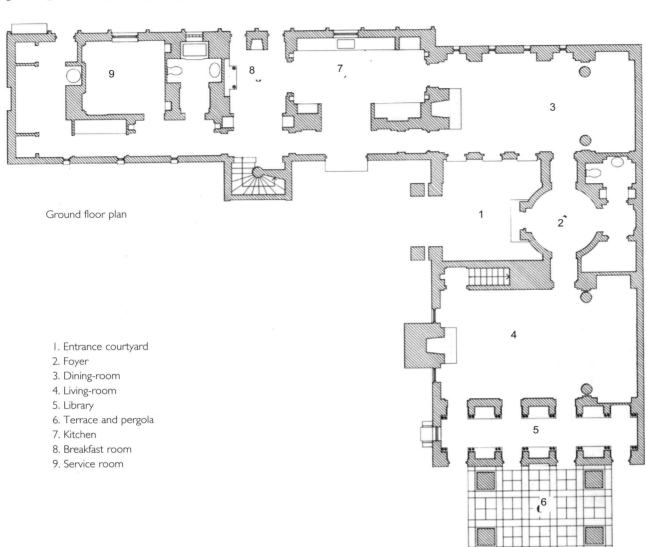

Ground floor plan

1. Entrance courtyard
2. Foyer
3. Dining-room
4. Living-room
5. Library
6. Terrace and pergola
7. Kitchen
8. Breakfast room
9. Service room

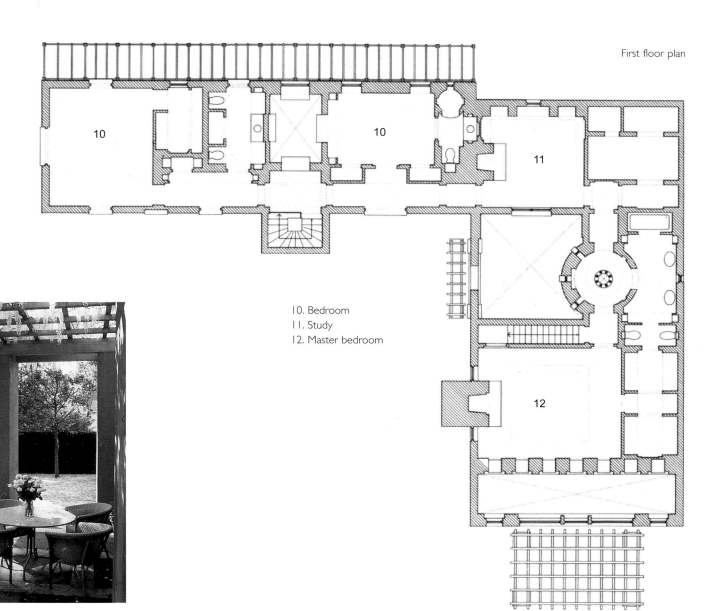

10. Bedroom
11. Study
12. Master bedroom

John Pawson
Maison Pawson

London, UK

This project was for the restoration of a dwelling in a Victorian terraced house in London. The façade of the building was left in its original state, except for the recession of the new entrance door leading to the raised ground floor where the two original reception rooms are transformed into one space. Here, both working fireplaces were retained.

A stone bench on the long wall acts as seating, hearth and light source. The interior atmosphere is minimal and comfortable. A table with benches and two chairs are the only furniture. On the opposite wall a row of pivoting doors conceals storage.

A new set of straight stairs lead to the bathroom. The bath, the floor, basin cube, and bench running around the edge of the room —which also contains the lavatory— are all made from the same cream colored stone. Gaps in the floor drain water from the shower mounted directly on the wall, and brimming over the edge of the bath. This is an attempt to capture some of the qualities with which bathing was once approached, more as a ritual than a hurried functional necessity.

On the same floor the two children's rooms have beds, shelves and desks in the same wood with corkboard forming one complete wall. The top floor, which is suffused with natural light, houses the main bedroom.

Materials are used as simply and directly as possible. The two white Carrara marble worktops, which are four inches thick and over fourteen feet long, are not mere surfaces, but elements in their own right. Holes have been cut into them for the marble sink and the iron cooking range.

Photographs: Richard Glover

With the exception of those that look onto the rear courtyard, the windows are made of etched glass. The kitchen was equipped with two large working areas made in Carrara marble.

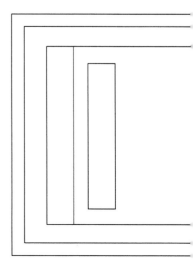

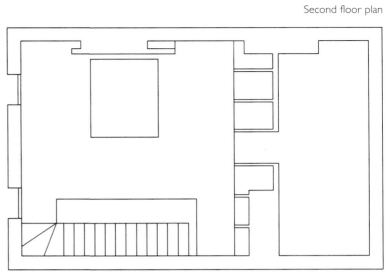

Second floor plan

First floor plan

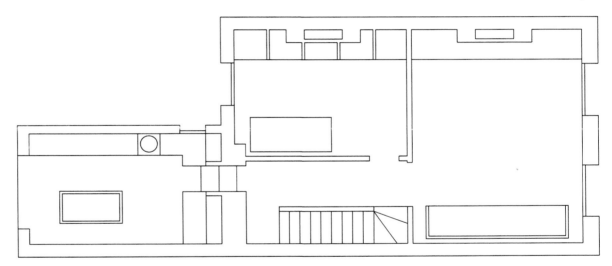

Ground floor plan

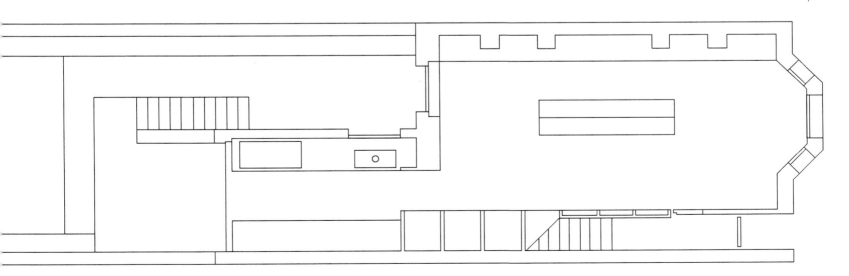

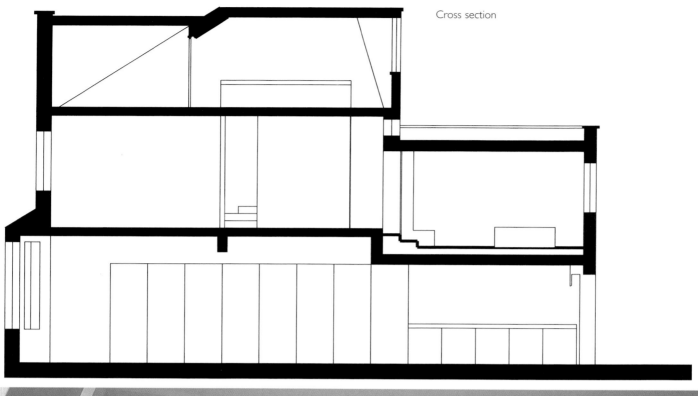

Cross section

In the bathroom, both the bathtub and the washbasin were made in stone of a soft cream colour. The floor and walls are clad in the same material.

Martin Wagner
Apartment Casa Sorée

Carona, Switzerland

In the renovation of Casa Sorée, each of the three apartments occupies a single floor, and the house´s three ground-level cellars form a single apartment.

Carona´s covered streets and porticos have been imitated in an interior street which connects the three existing storage cells.

This street extends directly from the ground-floor apartment´s main entrance, making the organization immediately apparent upon entry and allowing an extended view through the space. Following local tradition, the entry door opens into the kitchen. A new opening joins the kitchen to the existing covered portico for outdoor dining. The second of the apartment´s three rooms, used for living, opens to the pre-existing axis, which runs from the fireplace in the back wall outside.

The third room, for sleeping, includes a bathroom enclosed by a high, free-standing concrete wall which provides privacy and houses the necessary plumbing installations.

The design draws upon Carona´s history and built form and takes advantage of opportunities inherent within the existing structure to develop a unique layout for this dwelling.

Photographs: Reiner Blunck

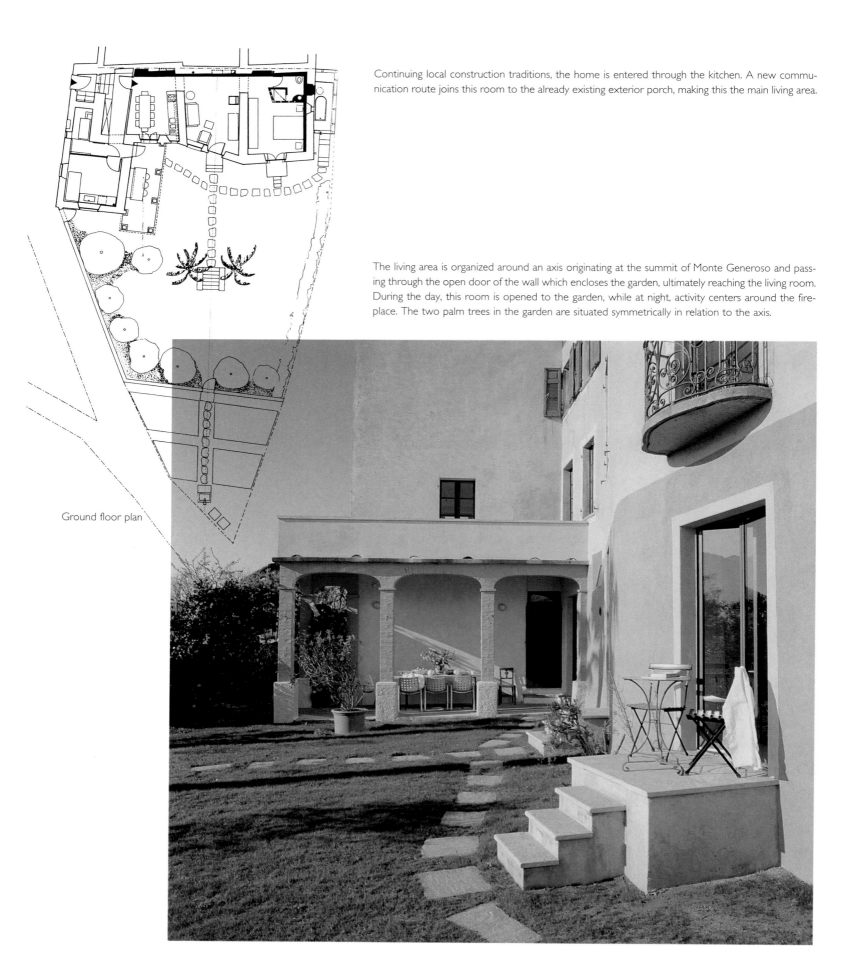

Continuing local construction traditions, the home is entered through the kitchen. A new communication route joins this room to the already existing exterior porch, making this the main living area.

The living area is organized around an axis originating at the summit of Monte Generoso and passing through the open door of the wall which encloses the garden, ultimately reaching the living room. During the day, this room is opened to the garden, while at night, activity centers around the fireplace. The two palm trees in the garden are situated symmetrically in relation to the axis.

Ground floor plan

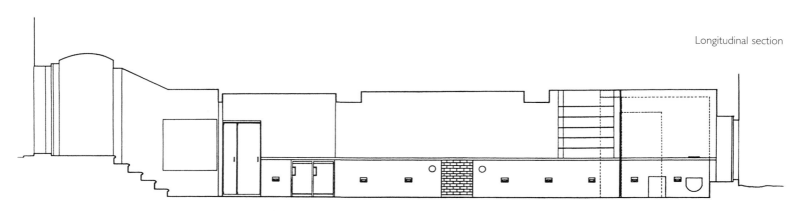

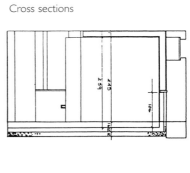

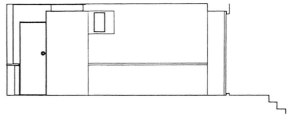

The night area has its own entrance from the garden and includes a bedroom and bath. The bathroom is enclosed within a bare concrete load-bearing wall which closes on itself and is separated from the roof by an almost imperceptible glass strip.

The concrete wall features tiny perforations in basic geometric shapes, thereby creating a relation to the attached dwelling while maintaining the feeling of privacy.

José Gigante
Wind Mill Reconversion

Vilar de Mouros/Caminha, Portugal

On the grounds of a recovered house in northern Portugal, an old abandoned windmill waited its turn to be useful again. In the course of time the idea finally arose of transforming this peculiar building into a small auxiliary dwelling belonging to the main house, giving it its own life and thus creating a completely inhabitable and independent space that could be used as a place of rest. For José Gigante, the presence of the mill was so strong that any major intervention would have minimized its charm. Therefore, without touching any of the thick granite walls, an unusual copper roof with a very gentle slope was added. The intention was to respect the memory of the place as far as possible, so the inspiration for the transformation began naturally from the inside out.

The layout and organization of the small space, with only 8 m² per floor, was not easy. Thanks to the choice of wood as the main building material, a welcoming atmosphere enhanced by the curved walls and the few openings was achieved.

On the lower floor, an impressive rock acts as an entrance step. Here, the intention was to achieve a minimum space in which different activities could be carried out. It houses a bathroom and a living room, with the possibility of transforming a small sofa into a curious bed: it is conceived as a case that contains all the necessary pieces for assembling the bed. On the upper floor, the furnishings are limited to a cupboard and a table/bed that is extended to the window.

The only openings are those that already existed in the mill and they have been left as they were conceived, with their natural capacity to reveal the exterior and to illuminate a space in which the contrasts between the materials cannot be ignored. The typology of this building was crucial to the restorations to which it has been subjected, and shows why the interior space is so important in this scheme. The thick circular walls occupy more space than the interior of the mill, but they hug the whole room and provide a welcoming and unconventional sensation that gives this building a new and innovative perspective.

Photographs: Luís Ferreira Alves

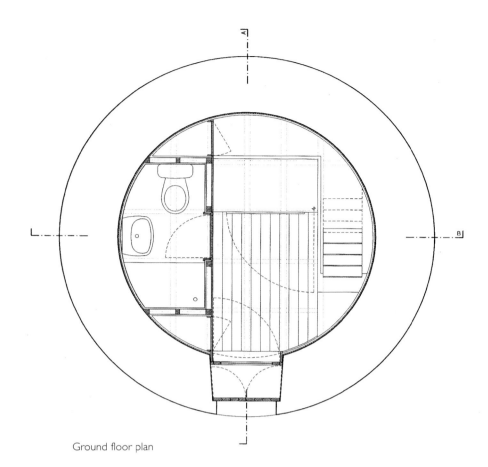

Ground floor plan

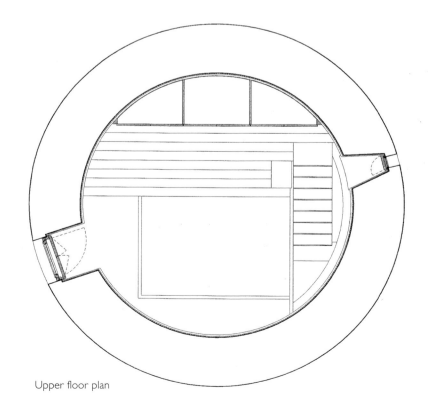

Upper floor plan

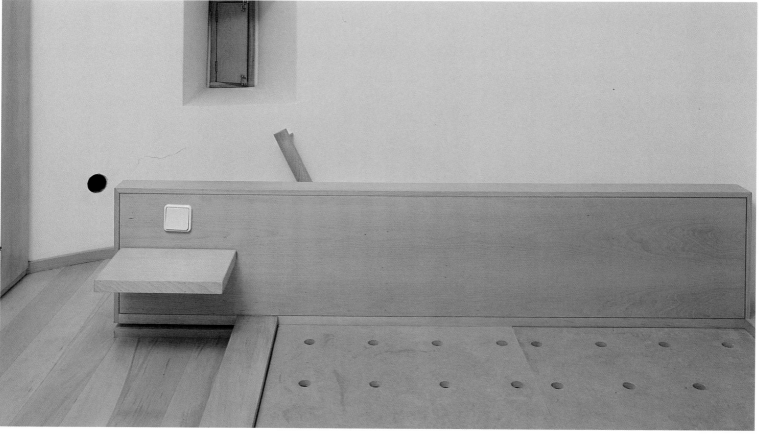

Markus Wespi & Jérôme de Meuron
House in Flawil

Flawil, Switzerland

Although not immediately visible from the exterior, a closer inspection of this house revealed that it was one of the first prefabricated timber constructions in Switzerland. It is located in an agricultural area where wood has been used extensively in building construction. The original outer rendering was entirely removed, to be replaced with slats of Douglas fir wood as exterior cladding and insulation all around the house. On the windowless facades, the slats have been placed closely together, while only every third slat was included on the south facade in order to let in views and light. Wood was also used extensively in the interior in order to create a sense of unity, while the roof was replaced with titanium-zinc sheeting.

Although the existing house was very small, the conversion extended it by only 1.5 meters to the south. In the process, the entire south facade was removed and replaced with large windows. Since the other three facades remained closed, the decision was made to harness some of the passive solar energy along the south facade.

A secondary road passes directly in front of the house, so the wooden slats provide a screen for preserving privacy, while also serving as solar protection in the summertime.

From a distance, the house seems to be a completely hermetic structure. In its simplicity, it is reminiscent of the traditional barns so common in this canton.

New insulation, central gas heating and a warm-air stack were installed. The original timber stud walls and concrete plinth were retained. The existing fir flooring on the upper floor was also retained, while parquet was added on the ground floor.

A covered bicycle stand and wood shelter are new additions in the garden.

Photographs: Hannes Henz

Section AA

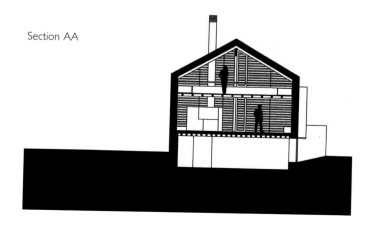

Section BB

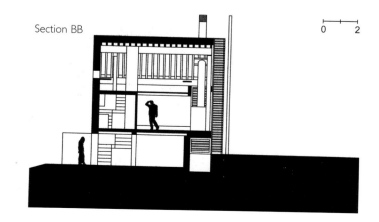

0　　2

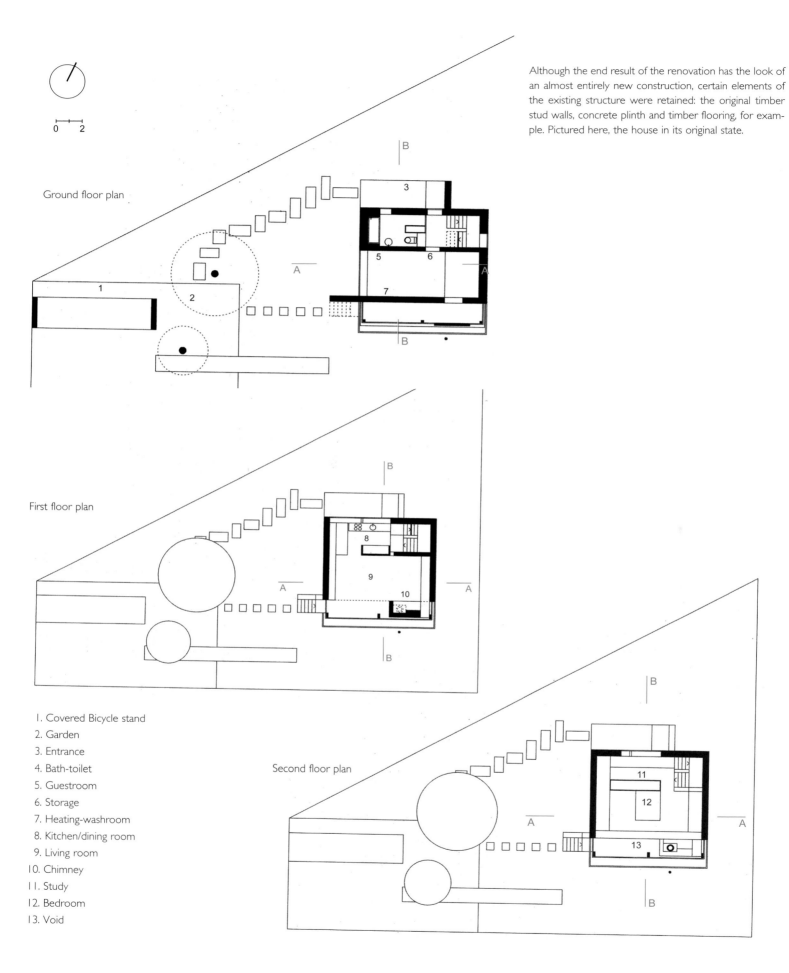

0   2

Ground floor plan

Although the end result of the renovation has the look of an almost entirely new construction, certain elements of the existing structure were retained: the original timber stud walls, concrete plinth and timber flooring, for example. Pictured here, the house in its original state.

First floor plan

Second floor plan

1. Covered Bicycle stand
2. Garden
3. Entrance
4. Bath-toilet
5. Guestroom
6. Storage
7. Heating-washroom
8. Kitchen/dining room
9. Living room
10. Chimney
11. Study
12. Bedroom
13. Void

The renovation involved creating a new front entrance, eliminating some of the windows and stripping the original structure's exterior rendering. The roof was replaced with titanium-zinc sheeting, while all exterior walls are clad in Douglas fir slats. The spacing of the slats on the south facade creates a sun shade and a screen for privacy within the home.

de Architectengroep
(Dick van Gameren
& Bjarne Mastenbroek)
Apartments in a sewage plant

Amsterdan, The Netherlands

In the garden city of Amsterdam-West, the concrete reservoir tanks of a former sewage plant have been converted into a housing project. Although the original master plan called for seven circular, urban villas on an open green strip between two neighborhoods, it was deemed much more interesting to juxtapose the site's raw, industrial elements with new dwellings, as opposed to relying on a blank slate to create a project with only a formal resemblance to the original elements.

The experiment of converting slurry tanks and pre-treatment facilities into housing and services for a new neighborhood offered the chance to give a unique signature to the development, something often lacking in new housing developments.

Three of the existing concrete drums were used – one was made into storage facilities for the adjacent dwellings; another was used as a gray water collection tank with an overflow leading to a nearby lake; and the third was converted into a small apartment building.30% of this last drum has been cut away in order to bring natural light into the apartments. The existing circular wall now serves as a screen between the new apartments and their immediate exterior surroundings. Each floor contains a three-room apartment and a small studio.Since the penthouse on top sits above the top of the wall of the concrete drum, it enjoys privileged 360-degree views of Amsterdam-West, the park and the lake. In contrast to this wide view, total privacy is achieved in the central living room by the absence of windows; instead, natural light filters through a skylight. All the other rooms, including a second living room, are situated along the perimeter. Movement through the building and apartments constantly shifts from completely introverted (the drum itself and the living room) to extroverted (all the other rooms, kitchen and terraces).

Photographs: Nicholas Kane

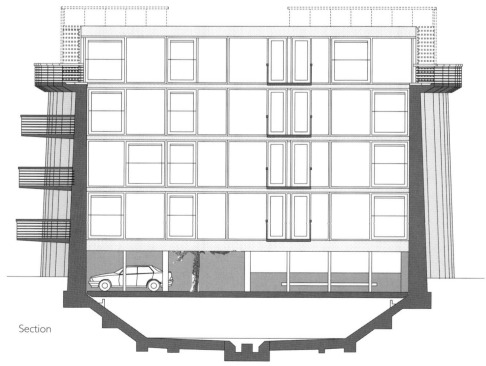

Section

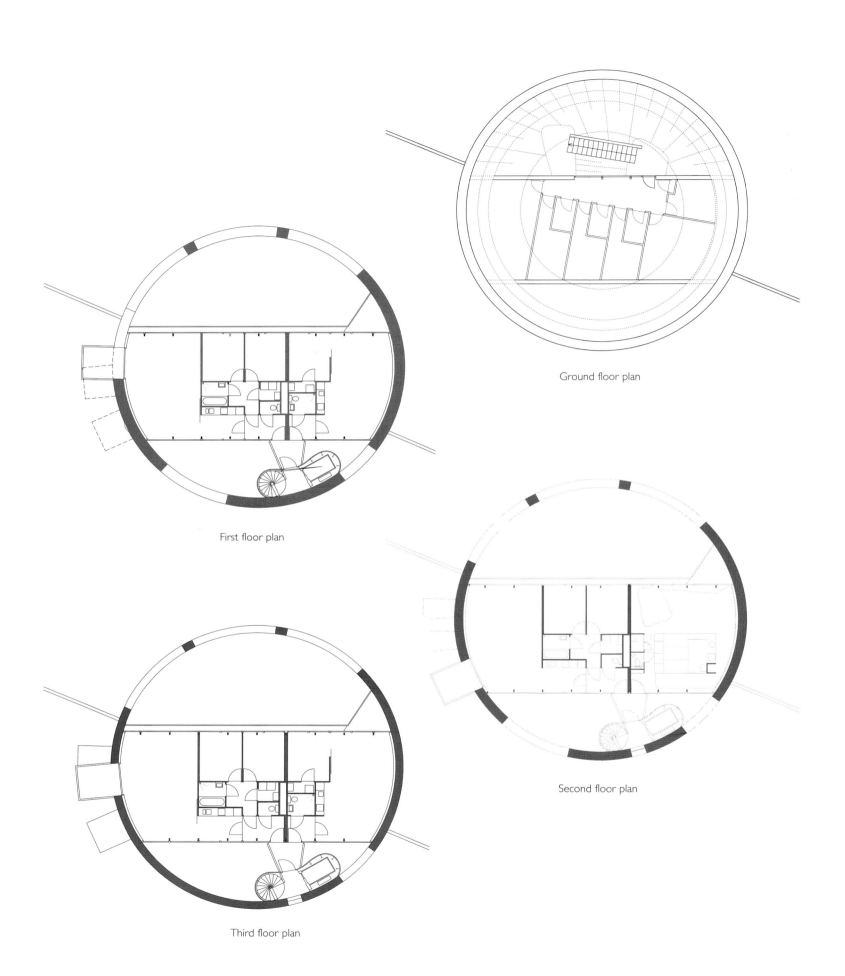

Ground floor plan

First floor plan

Second floor plan

Third floor plan

324

Penthouse floor plan

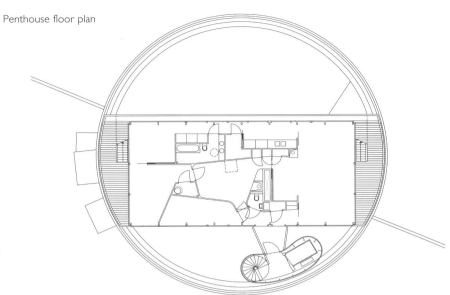

Of the three converted concrete drums, the one containing the dwellings has had 30% of its existing walls removed in order to bring natural light into the facade-side of the apartments and along the back, where each floor has a protruding balcony.

1. Balcony
2. Garden
3. Living-room
4. Utility room
5. Tatami room
6. Bathroom
7. Entrance
8. Studio

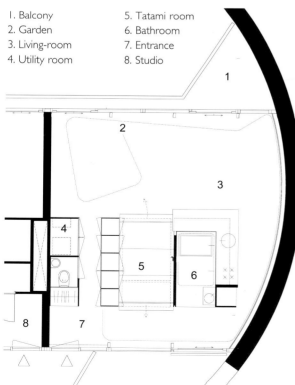

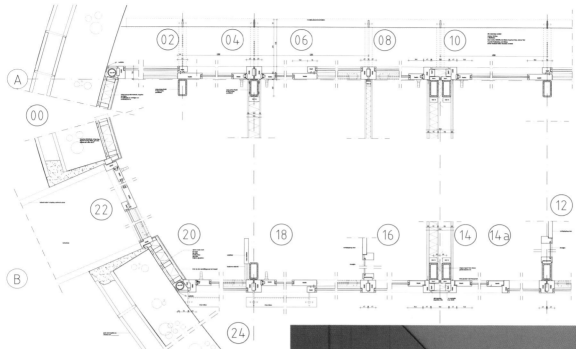

As seen on the opposite page, the building is accessed via a translucent, cylindrical shaft housing the elevator and stair. This volume stands independent of the building, yet within the concrete drum.

Jo Crepain Architect NV
Water-tower

Brasschaat, Belgium

Until 1937, this water tower with a height of over 23 meters was used to provide water to the castle and other buildings of the county of Brasschaat, near the city of Antwerp. After being in disuse for decades due to the construction of four new water tanks and the planning of a modern water supply system, it survived a planned demolition. The conservation of this peculiar cylindrical tower crowned by a large, four-metre-high cistern allowed it to be converted into an unusual single-family dwelling. The architect respected the original industrial typology, leaving the four large pillars that sustain the structure exposed, and also maintained the compositional structure and the essential functionality of the original design. This was achieved by minimizing the presence of decorative objects and by limiting the elements and materials to reinforced concrete, structural glass and galvanized metal. Around the original structure, a parallelepiped, double-height volume with a mezzanine surrounds the tower at ground level. This new construction houses the services and a living room that is totally open and transparent to the exterior. This breaks the verticality of the scheme and gains space, and its roof acts as a terrace for the first floor, which houses the main bedroom.

The new tower achieves its maximum expressiveness when it is illuminated at night. The transparency of the glass structure that wraps the building allows the occupants to enjoy the wooded landscape with a small winding creek and reveals the three floors of 4 m^2, each with a small balcony. These floors house, from bottom to top, the study, the guest bedroom and a small winter garden. At the top of the tower the water cistern is conserved, now transformed into a curious windowless space that is intended for private receptions.

Photographs: Sven Everaert / Ludo Noël

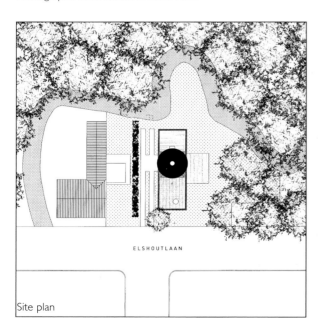

ELSHOUTLAAN

Site plan

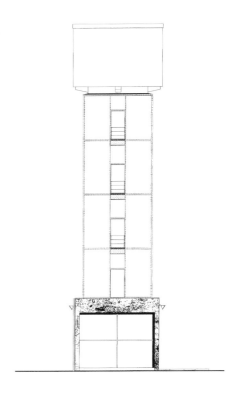

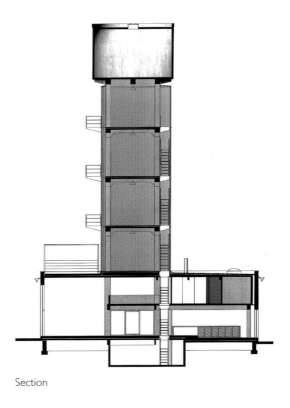

Section

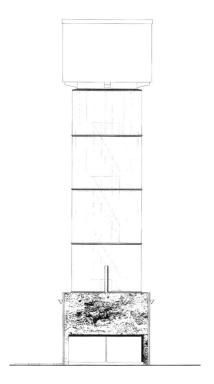

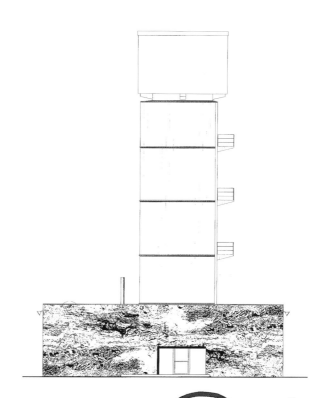

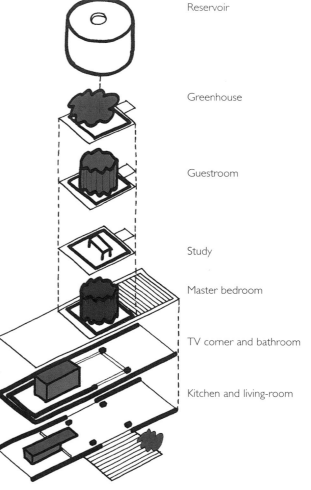

Reservoir

Greenhouse

Guestroom

Study

Master bedroom

TV corner and bathroom

Kitchen and living-room

From the front, this old water tower has a very similar appearance to that of the original building. At first sight, the glass and the galvanized metal seem to be the only incorporations to the structure.

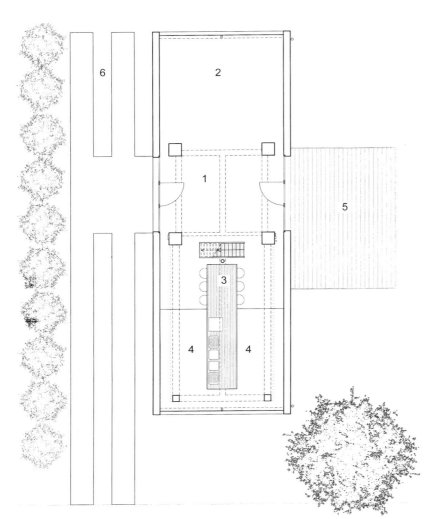
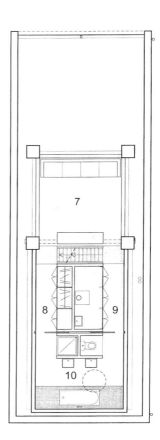

Floor plans

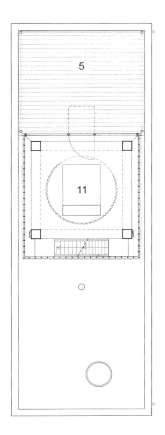

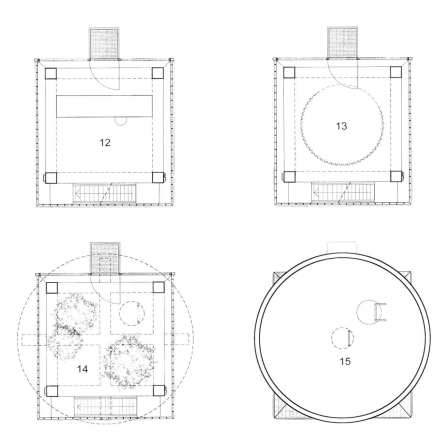

1. Entrance
2. Living-room
3. Dining
4. Kitchen
5. Terrace
6. Garage
7. TV-corner
8. Dressing
9. Storage
10. Bathroom
11. Bedroom
12. Study
13. Guestroom
14. Winter garden
15. Watertank

The construction of a larger volume on the first two floors, in which all the common areas and services are housed, breaks the spatial limitation of the rest of the floors and is the most striking feature of the tower.

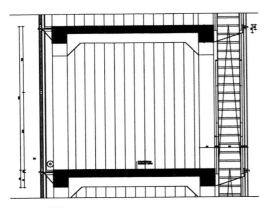

Section XX

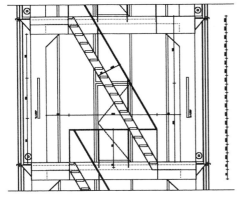

Section YY

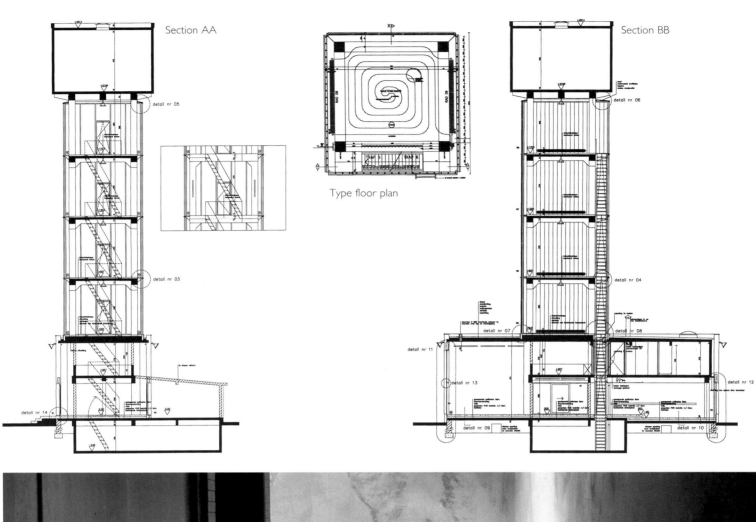

Section AA

detail nr 05

detail nr 03

detail nr 14

Type floor plan

Section BB

detail nr 06

detail nr 04

detail nr 07

detail nr 08

detail nr 11

detail nr 13

detail nr 12

detail nr 09

detail nr 10

Ogris : Wanek Architects
House isn

Klagenfurt, Austria

An inherited house, additions to the family and the adaptation of the building for modern needs formed the basis for the conversion and extension of an existing building. The building is of a typical post-WWII design that is so often seen in the vicinity. It is a well-rounded, proportioned and often underestimated type of construction, being very compact and balanced. When built, the house was reduced to the minimum standards of the day; now, its size is not adequate for a nuclear familiy's demands.

Any thoughtless extension of the volume would have affected the original formal air of the building. Hence, the architects sought to preserve the character of the house.

The development reacts to the conditions of the existing building and to the extension on the garden side, built in the 1960s. The volume of the south-facing development is only perceptible from the garden. The relation to the public space —with partial views of the new building from the street— can be described as self-confidently reserved.

In connection with the new garage section at the side there is a new structure that is charged with tension. Along with the existing building, it forms a composition of equal construction parts, yet from different times.

Photographs: Ferdinand Neumüller & the architects

Original elevation

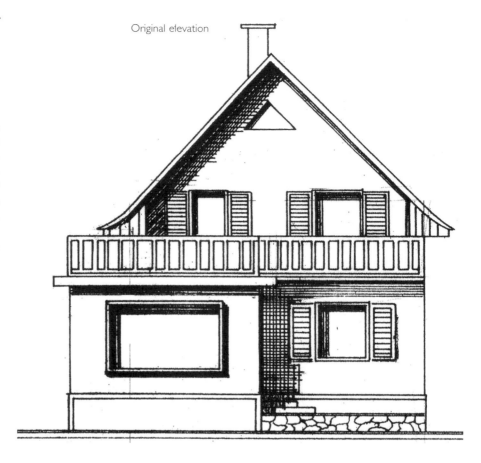

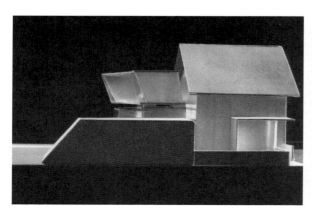

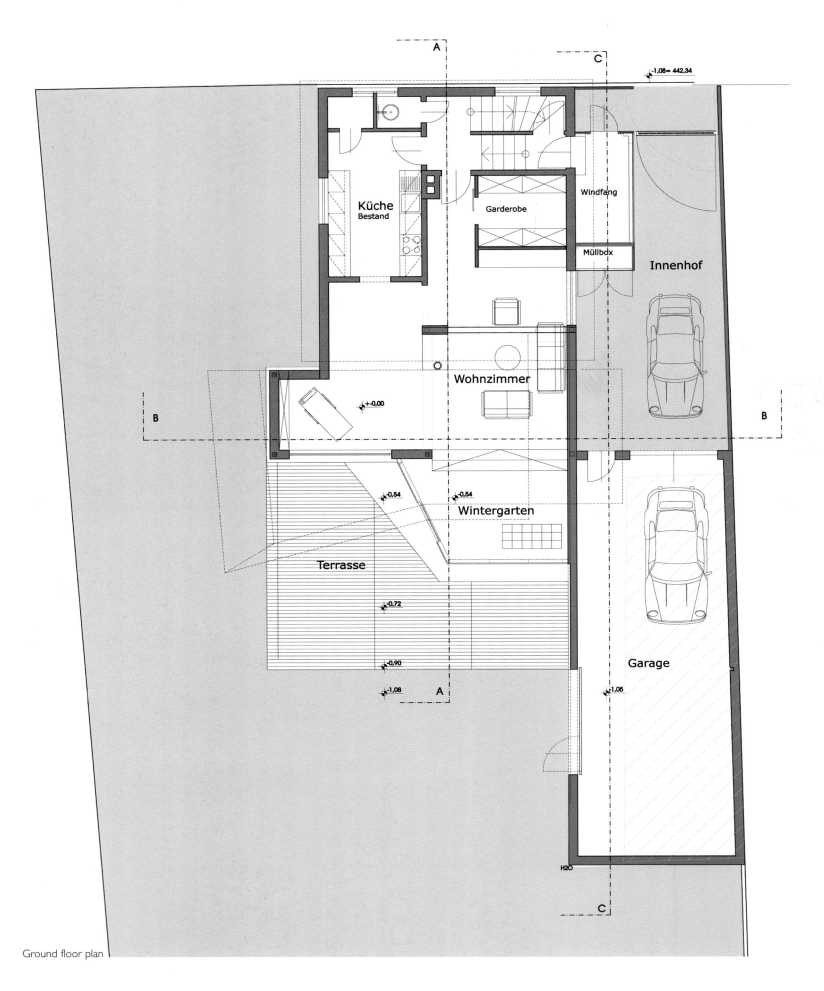

Küche
Bestand

Garderobe

Windfang

Müllbox

Innenhof

Wohnzimmer

Wintergarten

Terrasse

Garage

H2O

-1,08= 442,34

+0,00

-0,54

-0,54

-0,72

-0,90

-1,08

-1,05

A

B

C

A

B

C

Ground floor plan

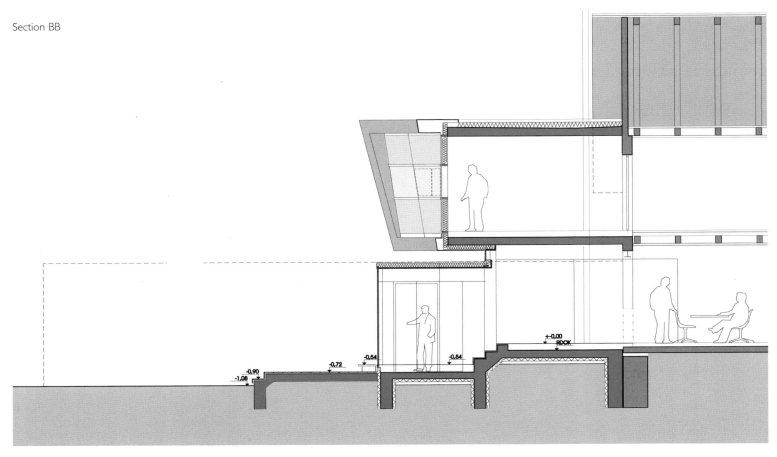

Jean Nouvel
Gasometer A

Wien, Austria

Architect Jean Nouvel's proposal to rehabilitate this gasometer was based on the conservation of the *genius loci* conception of the industrial monument, rebuilding the interior while creating a synergy between the weight of the walls and the new building structures; promoting a simpler vision, and at the same time bringing more light into the ensemble.

A simpler construction has been projected for this historic building to contrast with the grandiosity of the existing one. On the lower floors a skeleton of solid concrete gives way to the steel constructions of the upper levels, offering a lighter view. The interior reconstruction of gasometer A has been performed in 18 similar segments, which have been structured as housing towers, where the dwellings are divided into 9 independent blocks. The radial organization and the ravine-style separation between each block allow the inhabitants to enjoy open spaces. This openness is enhanced thanks to the light streaming in through wide internal windows, which make up the dwellings' main facade, and through the skylight covering the complex, as well as through the enormous windows in the ceramic wall of the old gasometer surrounding the building. Likewise, the side surfaces of the inter-block spaces are covered with sheets of stainless steel, reflecting the light from the skylight into the inner courtyard and contributing towards the luminosity of the complex.

On the lower floors of the cylinder there is a shopping center, which is surrounded by a hanging garden and covered by a crystal dome, which lets light into the shops below. The shopping center has a surface area of 5300m^2 occupying three floors, the uppermost of which is destined for night-time activities, replete with movie theaters and a concert hall.

Photographs: Philippe Ruault

Elevation module

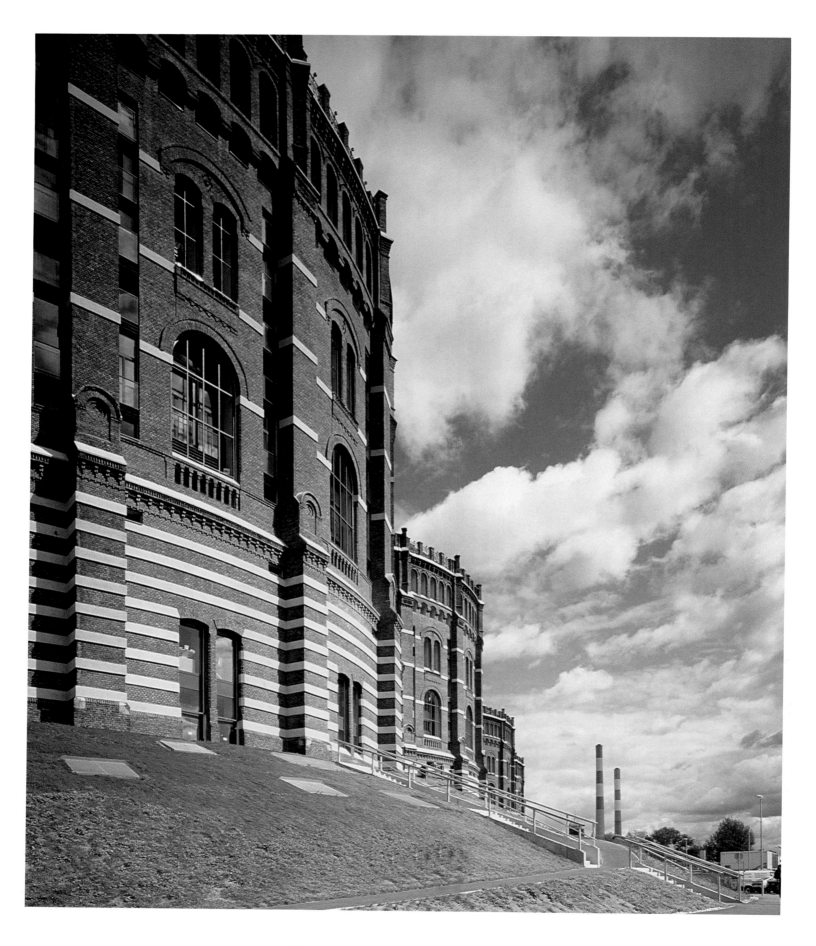

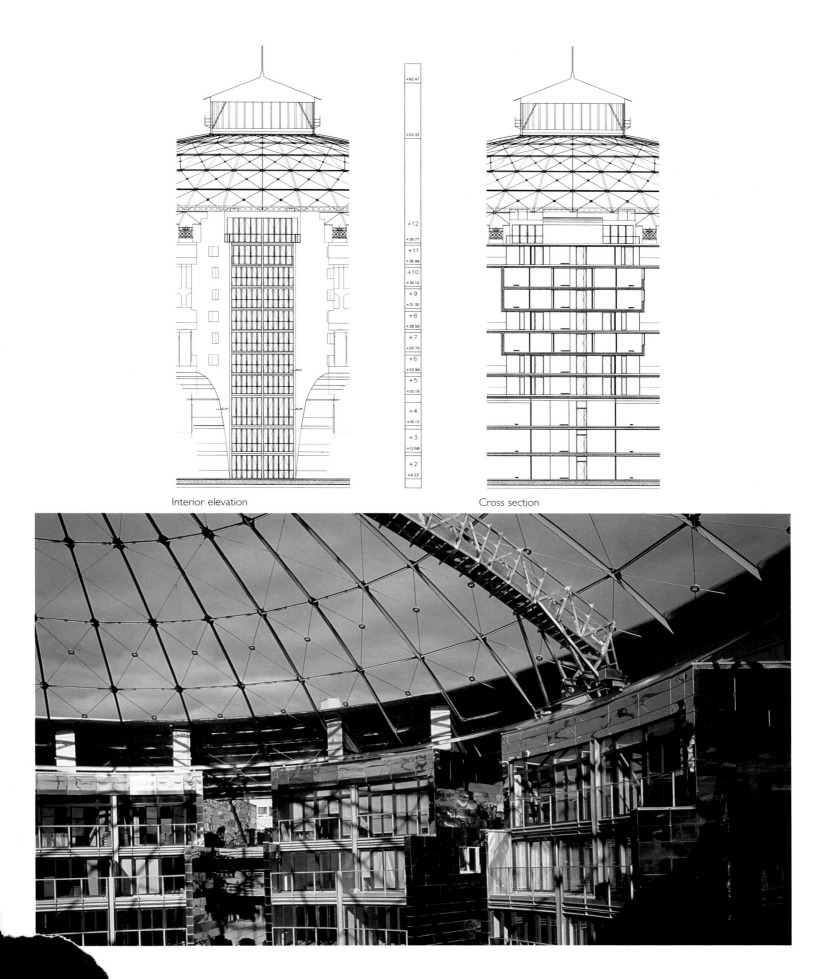

Interior elevation

+60.47

+53.33

+12
+39.77
+11
+36.99
+10
+34.10
+9
+31.30
+8
+28.59
+7
+25.70
+6
+22.99
+5
+20.19

+4
+16.13

+3
+12.68

+2
+9.23

Cross section

Ground floor plan

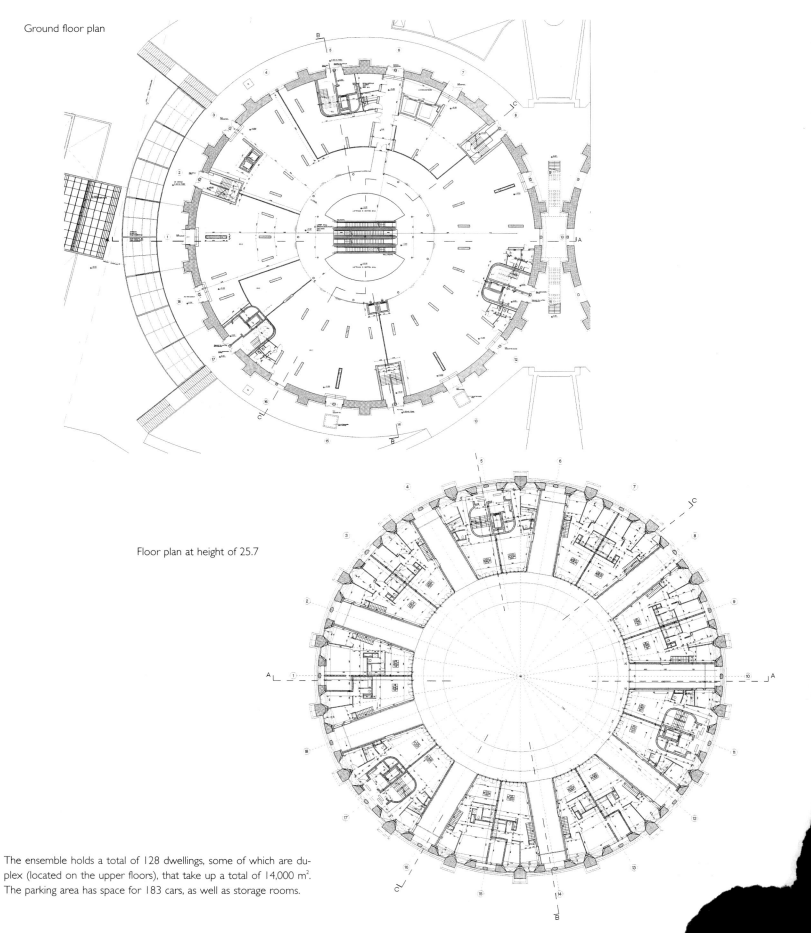

Floor plan at height of 25.7

The ensemble holds a total of 128 dwellings, some of which are duplex (located on the upper floors), that take up a total of 14,000 m². The parking area has space for 183 cars, as well as storage rooms.

Floor plan at height of 28.5

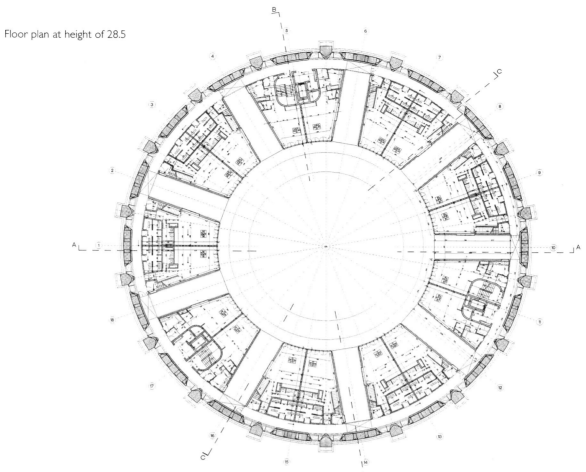

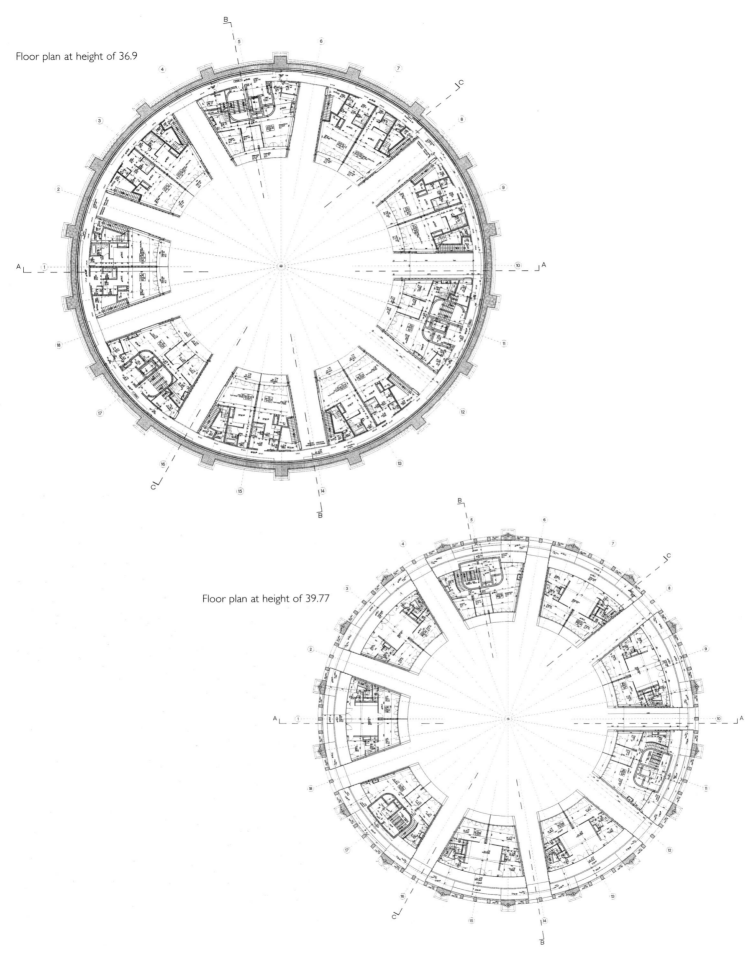

Floor plan at height of 36.9

Floor plan at height of 39.77

350

Roof floor plan

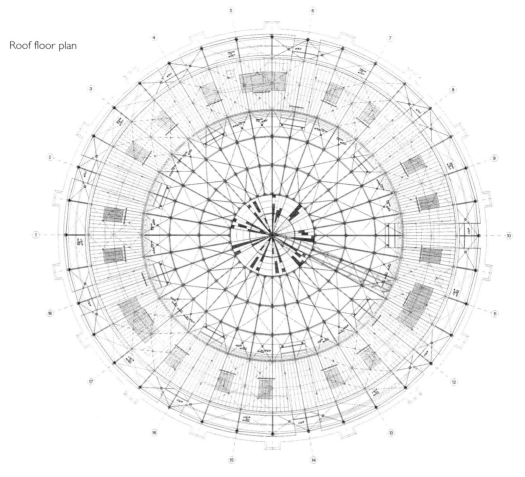

BB Section

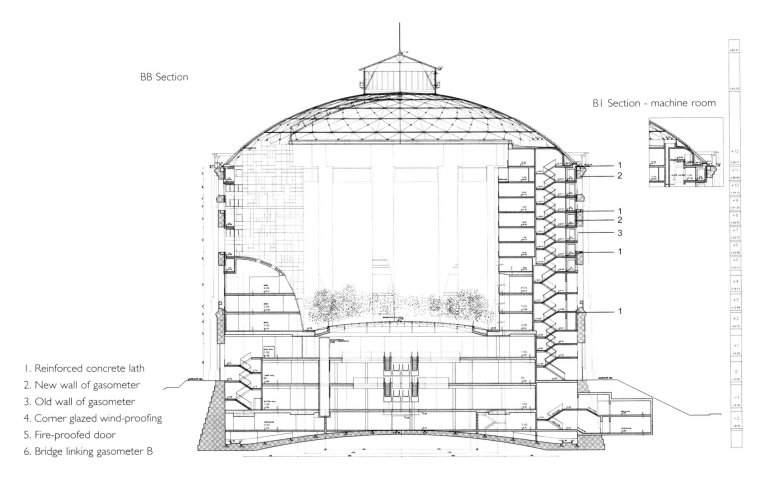

B1 Section - machine room

1. Reinforced concrete lath
2. New wall of gasometer
3. Old wall of gasometer
4. Corner glazed wind-proofing
5. Fire-proofed door
6. Bridge linking gasometer B

AA Section

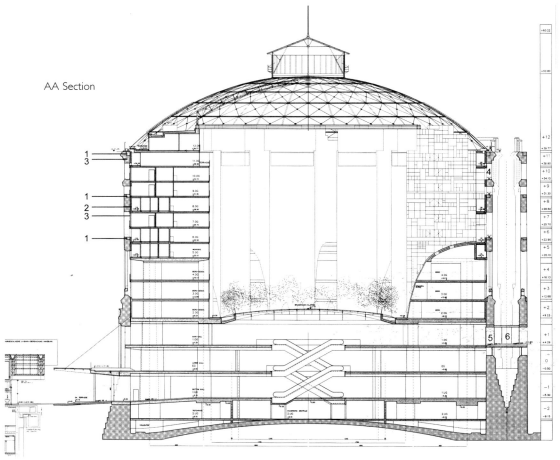

Beat Consoni
The Gnädinger house

St. Gallen, Switzerland

The Gnädiger house was built at the end of the last century. It is located in a forest near the city of St. Gallen. The building was in poor condition, so the facades needed restoration and there was a need for a new kitchen, a bathroom and central heating, as well as a new garage-workshop. The interior rooms were altered to meet current standards and requirements, without making changes to the structure and static construction means of the old house.

The new technical facilities, such as the kitchen and the bathroom, are concentrated in a compact unit, wich takes up a separate section horizonatally and vertically within the frame of the old stable The structures of this cube are kept separate from the house's original statics.

The floor plan of the garage-workshop is a square. This small building sets up a new relation between the ensemble and its surroundings. The construction is made of concrete, steel and glass. The main goal of the renovation of the old house was to reproduce construction techniques of yesterday using the materials and knowledge of today. The stable unit was originally built of large wooden boards, which were replaced with large bakelite-treated wooden boards.

The original façade covering, consisting of wooden shingles, was renewed with horizontal wood strips. The west façade, traditionally closed as a protection against wind and rain and originally covered with several-layers of wood-shingles, was given a new covering of translucent polycarbonate panels, allowing natural light to enter the building but at the same time not spoiling the character of this closed wall. With one true window and the original wood-clad wall underneath painted blue, the façade takes on a certain complexity, despite remaining a single unit.

Photographs: Markus Baumgartner

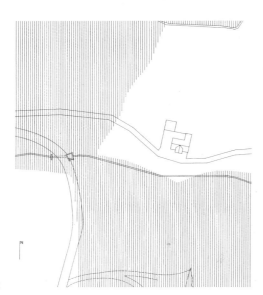

Site plan

354

355

The new pavilion, used as a garage and workshop, was built using only exposed concrete, steel and glass.

The construction of a new pavilion made it possible to establish a new type of relationship between the old building and the context in which it is located.

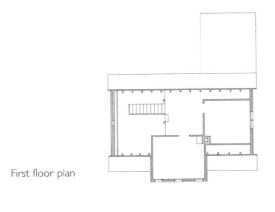

First floor plan

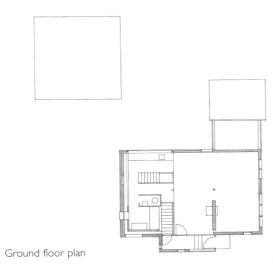

Ground floor plan

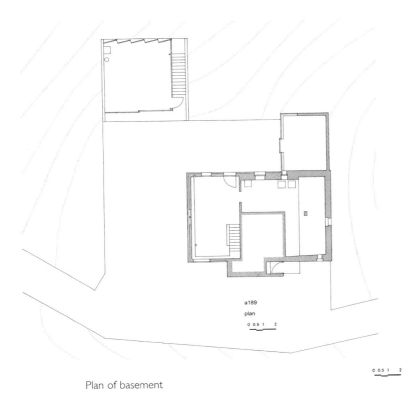

Plan of basement

a189
plan

0 0.5 1   2

0 0.5 1   2

357

The west facade was clad with translucent polycarbonate panels to maintain the idea of a closed facade without preventing the entrance of natural light.

Cross sections

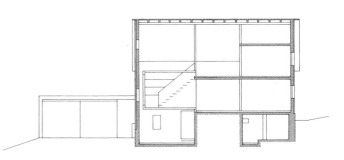